AMERICA
IN THE
LAST
DAYS

THE **CONSTITUTION** AND
THE **SIGNS** OF THE **TIMES**

MORRIS HARMOR

CFI
AN IMPRINT OF CEDAR FORT, INC.
SPRINGVILLE, UTAH

Because it is proper to take alarm at the first experiment on our liberties.
We hold this prudent jealousy to be the first duty of Citizens, and one of the
noblest characteristics of the late Revolution. The free men of America did not
wait till usurped power had strengthened itself by exercise, and entangled the
question in precedents. They saw all the consequences in the principle, and
they avoided the consequences by denying the principle.

James Madison, US Constitution, Amend. I, doc. 43.

ISBN 13: 978-1-4621-2023-9

Published by CFI, an imprint of Cedar Fort, Inc.
2373 W. 700 S., Springville, UT 84663
Distributed by Cedar Fort, Inc., www.cedarfort.com

LIBRARY OF CONGRESS CATALOGING-IN-PUBLICATION DATA

Names: Harmor, Morris, author.
Title: America in the last days : the Constitution and the signs of the times
   / Morris Harmor.
Description: Springville, Utah : CFI, an Imprint of Cedar Fort, Inc., [2017]
   | Includes bibliographical references and index.
Identifiers: LCCN 2017001608 (print) | LCCN 2017006446 (ebook) | ISBN
   9781462120239 (pbk. : alk. paper) | ISBN 9781462127795
Subjects: LCSH: Christianity and politics--Church of Jesus Christ of
   Latter-day Saints. | United States--History. | United States.
   Constitution. | Christianity and politics--United States--History. |
   Mormon Church--Doctrines. | Church of Jesus Christ of Latter-day
   Saints--Doctrines.
Classification: LCC BX8643.P6 H37 2017 (print) | LCC BX8643.P6 (ebook) | DDC
   261.7088/289332--dc23
LC record available at https://lccn.loc.gov/2017001608

Cover design by Kinsey Beckett
Cover design © 2017 by Cedar Fort, Inc.
Typeset by Rebecca Bird

Printed in the United States of America

10 9 8 7 6 5 4 3 2 1

Printed on acid-free paper

Contents

CONTENTS

For Mom and Dad, who taught me common sense,
common courtesy, an appreciation for eternal principles, and a
love for the liberty guaranteed by the Constitution of the United States.

For my wife, Barbara, and my children, Tyler, Travis, and
Teagan, who have endured this passion of mine.

For my grandchildren, who I hope will learn from this.

For our Founding Fathers, for their altruism, courage, integrity, and
diligence during that hot, humid, Philadelphia summer of 1787.

For the Book of Mormon prophets, who labored to preserve
their history, and their testimonies of our Savior, Jesus Christ.

For the Prophet Joseph Smith Jr., who, through his diligence and faithfulness,
translated the Book of Mormon and the book of Abraham, and received the
revelations contained in the Doctrine and Covenants.

For the Lord Jesus Christ, the ultimate defender of liberty.

ONE

Nephite Society Prior to the Second Coming

W e know that there will be great tumult and change before the Second Coming of our Lord. We often think of the wars, and rumors of wars, disease and pestilence, but these are not all we will experience. Other great changes will occur within our government and society.

President Ezra Taft Benson has referred to the Book of Mormon as "that which could give spiritual and intellectual unity to [our] whole life."[1] This is a very powerful statement to me: it is the Book of Mormon that allows us to integrate our spiritual principles with all aspects of our physical life, and allows us to have integrity in all that we do in church, in our intellectual pursuits, in our business dealings, and for our political beliefs. Integrity means to integrate your belief system so that it applies in all aspects of your life. President Benson also mentioned that "Every Latter-day Saint should make the study of this book a lifetime pursuit. Otherwise he is placing his soul in jeopardy."[2]

After explaining how the Book of Mormon is first "the keystone of our religion, . . . our witness of Christ . . . our doctrine [, and our] testimony,"[3] he proceeded to explain the second great purpose of the book:

The *second* great reason why we must make the Book of Mormon a center focus of study is that it was *written for our day*. The Nephites never had the book; neither did the Lamanites of ancient times. It was meant for us. Mormon wrote near the end of the Nephite civilization. Under the inspiration of God, who sees all things from the beginning, he abridged centuries of records, choosing the stories, speeches, and events that would be most helpful to us. . . . If they saw our day and chose those things which would be of greatest worth to us, is not that how we should study the Book of Mormon? We should constantly ask ourselves, "Why did the Lord inspire Mormon (or Moroni or Alma) to include that in his record? What lesson can I learn from that to help me live in this day and age?" And there is example after example of how that question will be answered. For example, in the Book of Mormon we find a pattern for preparing for the Second Coming. A major portion of the book centers on the few decades just prior to Christ's coming to America. . . . From the Book of Mormon we learn how disciples of Christ live in times of war. From the Book of Mormon we see the evils of secret combinations portrayed in graphic and chilling reality. In the Book of Mormon we find lessons for dealing with persecution and apostasy. We learn much about how to do missionary work. And more than anywhere else, we see in the Book of Mormon the dangers of materialism and setting our hearts on the things of the world. Can anyone doubt that this book was meant for us and that in it we find great power, great comfort, and great protection?[4]

This suggests that the Book of Helaman and the early chapters of 3 Nephi should be viewed carefully because, just as they illustrate the changes in society immediately prior to the Coming of the Savior to the Nephites, they also illustrate the changes we should expect to see in society immediately prior to His Second Coming. Let's take a close look at these chapters to see what changes will occur, or have already occurred, immediately prior to the Savior's return to usher in His millennial reign.

Helaman chapter 1 starts right off telling us about the "serious difficulty among the people" (verse 1) and the "serious contention concerning who should" (verse 2) be running their government, and that

CHAPTER ONE

this contention created "three divisions among the people" (verse 4). The leader of one of these groups, Paachi, was even "about to flatter away [his] people to rise up in rebellion" (verse 7) for he "sought to destroy the liberty of the people" (verse 8). Although he was tried and sentenced to death for his actions, one of his followers "murdered [the elected] Pahoran as he sat upon the judgement-seat" (verse 9). Now "because of [this] much contention and [this] much difficulty in the government, . . . they had not kept sufficient guards" (verse 18) in their capital city, which was Zarahemla, to guard against their enemies from attacking them.

In Helaman chapter 2, we learn that the secret band of men who protected Kishkumen by killing Pahoran the chief judge "had entered into a covenant that no one should know his wickedness" (verse 3). Gadianton then became the leader of this secret band and promised them "that if they would place him in the judgment-seat he would grant unto those who belonged to his band that they should be placed in power and authority [over] the people" (verse 5). We are informed that his object was "to murder, and also . . . the object of all those who belonged to his band to murder, and to rob, and to gain power, (and this was their secret plan, and their combination)" (verse 8).

The plan to kill Helaman, who was then the chief judge, was luckily thwarted. We learn of the significance of this band of Gadianton because they "did prove the overthrow, yea, almost the entire destruction of the people" (Helaman 2:13). It is also significant to learn that after peace was reestablished in the land that this was true except "all save it were the secret combinations which Gadianton the robber had established in the more settled parts of the land" (the urban areas) (Helaman 3:23).

Chapter 4 contains a great warning to us as members of The Church of Jesus Christ of Latter-day Saints:

> 11 Now this great loss of the Nephites, and the great slaughter which was among them, would not have happened had it not been for their wickedness and their abomination which was among them; yea, *and it was among those also who professed to belong to the church of God.*
> 12 it was because of the pride of their hearts, because of their exceeding riches, yea, it was because of their oppression to the

3

poor, withholding their food from the hungry, withholding their clothing from the naked, and smiting their humble brethren upon the cheek, making a mock of that which was sacred, denying the spirit of prophecy and of revelation, murdering, plundering, lying, stealing, committing adultery, rising up in great contentions, and deserting away into the land of Nephi, among the Lamanites—

13 And because of this their great wickedness, and their boastings in their own strength, they were left in their own strength; therefore they did not prosper, but were afflicted and smitten, and driven before the Lamanites, until they had lost possession of almost all their lands. (Helaman 4:11–13; emphasis added)

We are also informed "that they had altered and trampled under their feet the laws of Mosiah, or that which the Lord commanded him to give unto the people; and they saw that their laws had become corrupted, and that they had become a wicked people" (Helaman 4:22). We can liken the "laws of Mosiah, . . . which the Lord commanded him to give unto the people" (verse 22) to our own Constitution which was given to our Founding Fathers, and endorsed by the Lord. Chapter 5 tells us what eventually happened to their government, which was "established by the voice of the people" (Helaman 5:2).

2 For as their laws and their governments were established by the voice of the people, and they who chose evil were more numerous than they who chose good, therefore they were ripening for destruction, for the laws had become corrupted.

3 Yea, and this was not all; they were a stiffnecked people, insomuch that they could not be governed by the law nor justice. (Helaman 5:2–3)

Helaman chapter 6 tells us more about Gadianton's robbers and murderers saying, "there were many, even among the Nephites, of Gadianton's band" (Helaman 6:18) who "began to commit secret murders, and to rob and to plunder, that they might get gain" (verse 17), even to the point of murdering two chief judges as they "sat upon the judgement-seat" (verse 15). This was so serious that

> 21 The more part of the Nephites . . . did unite with those bands of robbers, and did enter into their covenants and their oaths, that they would protect and preserve one another in whatsoever difficult circumstances they should be placed, that they should not suffer for their murders, and their plunderings, and their stealings. 23 And thus they might murder, and plunder, and steal, and commit whoredoms and all manner of wickedness, contrary to the laws of their country and also the laws of their God.
> 24 And whosoever of those who belonged to their band should reveal unto the world of their wickedness and their abominations, should be tried, not according to the laws of their country, but according to the laws. (Helaman 6:21, 23–24)

During this time, the Lamanites were more righteous than the Nephites, "and they did preach the word of God among the more wicked part of them, insomuch that this band of robbers was utterly destroyed from among the Lamanites" (verse 37), but

> 38 On the other hand, . . . the Nephites did build them up and support them, beginning at the more wicked part of them, until they had overspread all the land of the Nephites, and had seduced the more part of the righteous until they had come down to believe in their works and partake of their spoils, and to join with them in their secret murders and combinations.
> 39 *And thus they did obtain the sole management of the government,* insomuch that they did trample under their feet and smite and rend and turn their backs upon the poor and the meek, and the humble followers of God.
> 40 And thus we see that they were in an awful state, and ripening for an everlasting destruction. (Helaman 6:38–40; emphasis added)

When we read these chapters, we must liken them to ourselves. The Nephites are analogous to the American people who have received their written Constitution from the hand of God. The Gadianton robbers are those who have the sole intent of obtaining the absolute management of our national government and promoting a policy of having all our substance in common. As we go on in chapter 7, we see that the

> 4 Gadianton robbers [were] filling the judgment-seats—having usurped the power and authority of the land; laying aside the commandments of God, and not in the least aright before him; doing no justice unto the children of men;
>
> 5 . . . letting the guilty and the wicked go unpunished because of their money; and moreover *to be held in office at the head of government*, to rule and do according to their wills, that they might *get gain and glory of the world*, and, moreover, that they might the more easily commit adultery, and steal, and kill, and *do according to their own wills*—
>
> 6 Now this great iniquity had come upon the Nephites, in the space of not many years. (Helaman 7:4–6; emphasis added)

Later on in the chapter, we learn why so many supported the Gadianton robbers: "Behold, it is to get gain, to be praised of men, yea, and that ye might get gold and silver. And ye have set your hearts upon the riches and the vain things of this world, for the which ye do murder, and plunder, and steal, and bear false witness against your neighbor, and do all manner of iniquity" (verse 21).

Now, we must remember here that government operates in *your* name and mine. If we allow these things to happen, or if we vote for individuals who promote policies to have all things in common using the force of government, or work to enact laws which destroy our inalienable, God-given rights to life, liberty, the ownership and control of property, and the ability to protect and defend them, then we are guilty of the murders, legal plunder, theft, and lies which they commit to stay in control of the government. This is made very clear in Doctrine and Covenants section 134: "We believe that governments were instituted of God for the benefit of man; and *that he holds men accountable for their acts in relation to them, both in making laws and administering them,* for the good and safety of society" (verse 1; emphasis added). This is especially true in our system where the people are sovereign and the government is only meant to protect their rights.

In Helaman chapter 7, the Lord declares:

> 25 Yea, wo be unto you because of that great abomination which has come among you; and ye have united yourselves unto it, yea, to that secret band which was established by Gadianton!
> 26 Yea, wo shall come unto you because of that pride which ye have suffered to enter your hearts, which has lifted you up beyond that which is good because of your exceedingly great riches! (Helaman 7:25–26)

Nephi adds his testimony, saying, "Behold, I know that these things are true because the Lord God has made them known unto me, therefore I testify that they shall be" (Helaman 7:29).

Are you looking for the works of the Gadiantons in our day? If we believe the Book of Mormon, shouldn't we be looking? Shouldn't we be studying the Constitution, as it was given and accepted by the Lord in 1833, to ensure that our political beliefs are compatible with that original document?

Helaman chapter 8 gives us a clear picture of how the Gadiantons operate once they have control of the government:

> 3 For behold, Nephi had spoken unto them concerning the corruptness of their law. . . .
> 4 And those judges were angry with him because he spake plainly unto them concerning their secret works of darkness. . . .
> 5. Therefore they did cry unto the people, saying: Why do you suffer this man to revile against us? . . .
> 6 We know that [the destruction of our people and cities] is impossible, for behold, we are powerful, and our cities great, therefore our enemies can have no power over us. . . .

7 Thus they did stir up the people to anger against Nephi, and raised contentions among them. (Helaman 8:3–7)

They feared to lay their hands on Nephi though because of those that believed his prophecies. Then Nephi tells them of the murder of their current chief judge, but the Gadiantons "caused that Nephi should be taken and bound and brought before the multitude, and they began to question him in divers ways that they might cross him, that they might accuse him to death" (Helaman 9:19). This is significant because just as Joseph Smith Jr. and Hyrum were murdered by the government of Illinois, the Gadiantons are trying to use government to "legally" murder Nephi. They even try to bribe him and promise him freedom saying, "Thou art confederate; who is this man that hath done this murder? Now tell us, and acknowledge thy fault; saying, Behold here is money; and also we will grant unto thee thy life if thou wilt tell us, and acknowledge the agreement which thou hast made with him" (verse 20). This sounds to me like our current witness protection system where we allow some felons to live freely and we pay them for their testimony against other felons.

Chapter 10 provides us with the result of all the contention among the people created by the Gadiantons (politicians): "There began to be contentions, insomuch that they were divided against themselves and began to slay one another with the sword" (Helaman 10:18). This sounds like what we are seeing in the news today with individual "special interest" groups who kill the police and the civilians in large cities.

Nephi, at this point, asks for a famine to be placed upon the land, and "the earth was smitten that it was dry, and did not yield forth grain in the season of grain" (Helaman 11:6). This caused the people to repent, "and they have swept away the band of Gadianton from amongst them insomuch that they have become extinct" (verse 10) and "the more part of the people, both the Nephites and the Lamanites, did belong to the church; and they did have exceedingly great peace in the land" (verse 21). But "in the space of not many years" (verse 26), dissenters arose among the Nephites who caused the Lamanites to "[commence] a war with their brethren" (verse 24) and they "became an exceedingly great band of robbers; and they did search out all the secret plans of Gadianton; and thus they became robbers of Gadianton" (verse 26). Meanwhile, the Nephites "began again to forget the Lord their God. And . . . to wax strong in iniquity. . . . And . . . they did wax stronger and stronger in their pride, and in their wickedness; and thus they were ripening again for destruction" (verse 37). In our terms, we could think in terms of election cycles where we may feel happy with the results of one election but may see a complete turnaround in the next election. A statement, often attributed to Thomas Jefferson but actually made by John Philpot Curran, applies here: "The condition upon which God hath given liberty to man is eternal vigilance; which condition if he break, servitude is at once the consequence of his crime and the punishment of his guilt." This is most commonly quoted as: "Eternal vigilance is the price of liberty."[5]

In Helaman chapter 13, Samuel the Lamanite asked the Nephites a question appropriate for us today: "O ye . . . hardened and ye stiff-necked people, how long will ye suppose that the Lord will suffer you? *Yea, how long will ye suffer yourselves to be led by foolish and blind guides?* Yea, how long will ye choose darkness rather than light?" (Helaman 13:29; emphasis added).

Then, in 3 Nephi 1:3, we find Nephi leaving the land "and whither he went, no man knoweth" and leaving records with his son Nephi. During this time,

> 4 The prophecies of the prophets began to be fulfilled more fully; for there began to be greater signs and greater miracles wrought among the people.
> 5 But there were some who began to say that the time was past for the words to be fulfilled, which were spoken by Samuel, the Lamanite.
> 7 And . . . they did make a great uproar throughout the land; . . .
> 9 [And they caused that] there was a day set apart by the unbelievers, that all those who believed in those traditions should be put to death except the sign should come to pass, which had been given by Samuel the prophet. (3 Nephi 1:4–5, 7, 9)

Now this requires some thought on our part: who were the people who were going to "put to death" the believers? Were they roving gangs of criminals? Were they the neighbors of the believers? Or was it the constituted government that was going to do this in a "legal" manner. In any case, the believers were saved by the sign promised by Samuel, for

> 19 There was no darkness in all that night, but it was as light as though it was mid-day. And . . . the sun did rise in the morning again, according to its proper order; and they knew that it was the day that the Lord should be born, because of the sign which had been given.
>
> 21 And it came to pass also that a new star did appear, according to the word. (3 Nephi 1:19, 21)

After this, people believed and converted, "save it were for the Gadianton robbers, who dwelt upon the mountains, who did infest the land; for so strong were their holds and their secret places that the people could not overpower them; therefore they did commit many murders, and did do much slaughter among the people" (3 Nephi 1:27). Now to make things worse, "they had many children who did grow up and began to wax strong in years . . . and were led away by . . . [the] lyings and . . . [the] flattering words, to join those Gadianton robbers. And thus were the Lamanites afflicted also, and began to decrease as to their faith and righteousness, *because of the wickedness of the rising generation*" (verses 29–30; emphasis added). Is it more or less to give eighteen-year-olds the right to vote?

In 3 Nephi chapter 2, we see that within a space of only ten years after the great sign of the Savior's birth was given, the "people did still remain in wickedness, notwithstanding the much preaching and prophesying which was sent among them" (3 Nephi 2:10). In the thirteenth year, "the Gadianton robbers had become so numerous, and did slay so many of the people, and did lay waste so many cities, and did spread so much death and carnage throughout the land, that it became expedient that all the people, both the Nephites and the Lamanites, should take up arms against them. Therefore, all the Lamanites who had become converted unto the Lord did unite with their brethren, the Nephites, and were compelled, for the safety of their lives and their women and their children, to take up arms against those Gadianton robbers" (verses 11–12). What was it that they were trying to protect from the Gadiantons? They took up arms to "maintain their rights, and the privileges of their church and of their worship, and their freedom and their liberty" (verse 12). It is interesting see the cause of the Gadiantons' success: it was "because of the wickedness of the people . . . and their *many contentions and dissensions*, the Gadianton robbers did gain many advantages over them" (verse 18). Doesn't this describe well our present situation in society?

In chapter 3 of 3 Nephi, Giddianhi, the leader of the Gadiantons, writes a letter to Lachoneus, the governor of the Nephites, demanding that the Nephites surrender. Lachoneus refuses and appoints Gidgiddoni, "a great prophet among them" (3 Nephi 3:19), to be captain of the army. The people in their righteous indignation then ask Gidgiddoni to "Pray unto the Lord, and let us go up upon the mountains and into the wilderness, that we may fall upon the robbers and destroy them in their own lands" (verse 20). Does this sound familiar? We now call it "preemptive war," instead of the offensive war that it is. Listen to how Gidgiddoni responds to them: "The Lord forbid; for if we should go up against them the Lord would deliver us into their hands; . . . we will not go against them, but we will wait till they shall come against us; therefore as the Lord liveth, if we do this he will deliver them into our hands" (verse 21). We see this again when Mormon refuses to lead the Nephites in an offensive war. This relates to our world situation today where we, the citizens of the United States, have somehow allowed our leaders to wage offensive wars in foreign lands, many believing this to be appropriate. Gidgiddoni then prepares the people to fight a very effective defensive war and "[causes] that they should make weapons of war of every kind, and they should be strong with armor, and with shields, and with bucklers, after the manner of his instruction" (verse 26).

Once in battle, Gidgiddoni had no moral difficulty with preventing the retreat of the enemy, or slaying any enemy combatant who refused to be taken prisoner, or hanging the enemy leader up on a tree until he was dead (see 3 Nephi 4:27–28).

I believe these are political lessons we can learn from the Book of Mormon. We can even take a lesson from the way they handled prisoners: "When they had taken all the robbers prisoners, insomuch that none did escape who were not slain, they did cast their prisoners into prison, and did cause the word of God to be preached unto them; and as many as would repent of their sins and enter into a covenant that they would murder no more were set at liberty" (3 Nephi 5:4). Such an arrangement would certainly be worth a try since a study was released in 2012 reporting that "in 2010 in the forty states that participated [in the study], the annual average taxpayer cost in these states was $31,286 per inmate."[6]

Lachoneus and Gidgiddoni established order in the land after the war ended, and we are told that "they had formed their laws according to equity and justice" (3 Nephi 6:4). But once again,

> 10 There began to be some disputings among the people; and some were lifted up unto pride and boastings because of their exceedingly great riches, yea, even unto great persecutions;
> 11 For there were many merchants in the land, and also many lawyers, and many officers.
> 12 And the people began to be distinguished by ranks, according to their riches and their chances for learning; yea, some were ignorant because of their poverty, and others did receive great learning because of their riches.
> 14 And thus there became a great inequality in all the land, insomuch that the church began to be broken up. (3 Nephi 6:10–12, 14)

Mormon goes on to tell us the cause of this iniquity among the people, saying, "Satan had great power, unto the stirring up of the people to do all manner of iniquity, and *to the puffing them up with pride, tempting them to seek for power, and authority*, and riches, and the vain things of the world" (3 Nephi 6:15; emphasis added).

At this time, we are told,

> 20 There began to be men inspired from heaven and sent forth, standing among the people in all the land, preaching and testifying boldly of the sins and iniquities of the people, . . .
>
> 21 [but] there were many of the people who were exceedingly angry because of those who testified of these things; and those who were angry were chiefly the chief judges, and they who had been high priests and lawyers; yea, all those who were lawyers were angry with those who testified of these things.
>
> 23 [And] there were many of those who testified of the things pertaining to Christ who testified boldly, who were taken and put to death secretly by the judges, . . .
>
> 24 [which] was contrary to the laws of the land, that any man should be put to death except they had power from the governor of the land. (3 Nephi 6:20–21, 23–24)

These judges were taken and brought before the chief judge "to be judged of the crime which they had done, according to the law which had been given by the people" (3 Nephi 6:26). The efforts to try these judges were thwarted, however, by the judges' families and friends who

> 28 Did enter into a covenant one with another, yea, even into that covenant which was given by them of old, which covenant was . . . administered by the devil. . . .
>
> 29 Therefore they did combine against the people of the Lord, and enter into a covenant to destroy them, and to deliver those who were guilty of murder from the grasp of justice, which was about to be administered according to the law.
>
> 30 And they did set at defiance the law and the rights of their country; and they did covenant one with another to destroy the governor, and to establish a king over the land, that the land should no more be at liberty but should be subject unto kings. (3 Nephi 6:28–30)

The Gadiantons were not successful in establishing a king, but they did cause the people to "divide one against another; and . . . separate one from another into tribes" (3 Nephi 7:2). This, of course, resulted in "the regulations of the government [being] destroyed, because of the secret combination . . . [which] did cause a great contention in the land" (verses 6–7). These tribes were "not united as to their laws, and their manner of government, for they were established according to the minds of those who were their chiefs and their leaders. But they did establish very strict laws that one tribe should not trespass against another, insomuch that in some degree they had peace in the land" (verse 14).

President Benson taught,

> The history of nations shows that the cycle of the body politic slowly but surely undergoes change. It progresses—From bondage to spiritual faith—From spiritual faith to courage—From courage to freedom—From freedom to abundance—From abundance to selfishness—From selfishness to complacency—From complacency to apathy—From apathy to fear—From fear to dependency—From dependency to bondage.[7]

This being the case, where do you see the United States along the path? It seems to me that we have allowed our leaders to cause us to live in fear of terrorists, while they do little to stop terrorists from entering into the country. While our government may not always be ideal or correct, we can learn to not fall into the sinusoidal cycle, and follow President Benson's guidance instead.

"Obamacare has pushed us over the entitlements tipping point. In 2011 some 49.2 percent of U.S. households received benefits from one or more government programs—about 151 million out of an estimated 306.8 million Americans—according to U.S. Census Bureau data released last October." And with the ranks of Obamacare growing, "52 percent of U.S. households—more than half—now receive benefits from the government. . . . As Benjamin Franklin reportedly said, 'When the people find that they can vote themselves money, that will herald the end of the republic.' They learned that from the 2008 election and turned out in big numbers again in 2012."[8]

CHAPTER ONE

A similar principle, attributed to Aristotle, says, "Republics decline into democracies and democracies degenerate into despotisms."

In 3 Nephi, the Lord Himself explains the reason for the destruction of a great Nephite city, saying,

> And behold, that great city Jacobugath, which was inhabited by the people of king Jacob, have I caused to be burned with fire because of *their sins and their wickedness, which was above all the wickedness of the whole earth, because of their secret murders and combinations; for it was they that did destroy the peace of my people and the government of the land*; therefore I did cause them to be burned, to destroy them from before my face, that the blood of the prophets and the saints should not come up unto me any more against them. (3 Nephi 9:9; emphasis added)

Moroni makes some final comments directly to us, the Gentiles on the American continent, after describing the utter destruction of the Jaredites in Ether chapter 8; he says,

> 21 And they [the secret combinations] have caused the destruction of this people of whom I am now speaking, and also the destruction of the people of Nephi.
> 22 And whatsoever nation shall uphold such secret combinations, to get power and gain, until they shall spread over the nation, behold, they shall be destroyed; for the Lord will not suffer that the blood of his saints, which shall be shed by them, shall always cry unto him from the ground for vengeance upon them and yet he avenge them not.
> 23 Wherefore, O ye Gentiles [that's us], it is wisdom in God that these things should be shown unto you, that thereby ye may repent of your sins, and suffer not that these murderous combinations shall get above you, which are built up to get power and gain—and the work, yea, even the work of destruction come upon you, yea, even the sword of the justice of the Eternal God shall fall

15

upon you, to your overthrow and destruction if ye shall suffer these things to be.

24 Wherefore, *the Lord commandeth you*, when ye shall see these things come among you that *ye shall awake to a sense of your awful situation*, because of this secret combination *which shall be among you*. . . .

25 For it cometh to pass that whoso buildeth it up seeketh to *overthrow the freedom of all lands, nations, and countries;* and it bringeth to pass the destruction of all people, for it is built up by the devil, who is the father of all lies; even that same liar who beguiled our first parents, yea, even that same liar who hath caused man to commit murder from the beginning; who hath hardened the hearts of men that they have murdered the prophets, and stoned them, and cast them out from the beginning. (Ether 8:21–25; emphasis added)

NOTES

1. Ezra Taft Benson, "The Book of Mormon Is the Word of God," *Ensign*, May 1975.
2. Ibid.
3. Ezra Taft Benson, "The Book of Mormon—Keystone of Our Religion," *Ensign*, November 1986.
4. Ibid.
5. Suzy Platt, ed., *Respectfully Quoted: A Dictionary of Quotations* (Washington, D.C.: CQ Press, 1992), 200.
6. Marc Santora, "City's Annual Cost Per Inmate Is $168,000, Study Finds," *The New York Times*, August 23, 2013, http://www.nytimes.com/2013/08/24/nyregion/citys-annual-cost-per-inmate-is-nearly-168000-study-says.html?_r=0.
7. Ezra Taft Benson, "This Nation Shall Endure" (Brigham Young University speech, December 4, 1973); speeches.byu.edu.
8. Merrill Matthews, "We've Crossed the Tipping Point; Most American's Now Receive Government Benefits," *Forbes*, July 2, 2014, http://www.forbes.com/sites/merrillmatthews/2014/07/02/weve-crossed-the-tipping-point-most-americans-now-receive-government-benefits/#3f9738016233.

TWO

Our Society Prior to the Second Coming

Though the Book of Mormon warns us against following foolish and blind guides, we can only recognize these guides *if* we understand the Constitution as it was endorsed by the Lord in 1833. In Doctrine and Covenants section 98, the Lord instructs Joseph Smith:

> And now, verily I say unto you concerning the laws of the land, it is my will that my people should observe to do all things whatsoever I command them.
>
> And that law of the land which is constitutional, supporting that principle of freedom in maintaining rights and privileges, belongs to all mankind, and is justifiable before me.
>
> Therefore, I, the Lord, justify you, and your brethren of my church, in befriending that law which is the constitutional law of the land;
>
> And as pertaining to law of man, *whatsoever is more or less than this, cometh of evil.* (D&C 98:4–7; emphasis added)

From these verses, we see that the Lord endorsed the Constitution as an inspired document *as it stood in 1833.* Because there has been a multitude of changes to it since then, and it is up to us to discover "whatsoever is more or less than this," it is the purpose of this book to explore the changes that have been made to the Constitution and to our system of government built around it to see if those changes are not only by the Spirit but also by the letter of the Constitution given to us by our forefathers and endorsed by the Lord. The Lord tells us in Helaman 15 that we must be "firm and steadfast in the faith, and in the thing wherewith they have been made free" (verse 8).

So, let's look into our "awful situation" and see where we, as a people, have gone wrong; where we have allowed the Constitution to become convoluted. This will help ourselves to remove from ourselves any guilt for ignorantly sinning, and better prepare us to receive the Lord when He comes in glory. The format I will use in this book is one where I try to say very little but provide you with the understanding, meaning, and intention of our Founding Fathers through direct quotations from them on each of the subjects we explore.

SAMUEL ADAMS

The liberties of our Country, the freedom of our civil constitution are worth defending at all hazards: And it is our duty to defend them against all attacks. We have receiv'd [sic] them as a fair Inheritance from our worthy Ancestors. They have purchas'd [sic] them for us with toil and danger and expence [sic] of treasure and blood; and transmitted them to us with care and diligence. It will bring an everlasting mark of infamy on the present generation, enlightened as it is, if we should suffer them to be wrested from us . . . without a struggle; or be cheated out of them by the artifices of false and designing men. Of the latter we are in most danger at present: Let us therefore be aware of it. Let us contemplate our forefathers and posterity; and resolve to maintain the rights bequeath'd [sic] to us from the former, for the sake of the latter. . . . Let us remember, that "if we suffer tamely a lawless attack upon our liberty, we encourage it, and involve others in our doom." It is a very serious consideration, which should deeply impress our minds, that millions yet unborn may be the miserable sharers of the event.[1]

CHAPTER TWO

PATRICK HENRY

That government is no more than a choice between evils, is acknowledged by the most intelligent among mankind, and has been a standing maxim for ages.[2]

The great and direct end of government is liberty. Secure our liberty and privileges, and the end of government is answered.[3]

THOMAS PAINE

Society in every state is a blessing, but government, even in its best state is but a necessary evil; in its worst state an intolerable one; for when we suffer or are exposed to the same miseries by a government, which we might expect in a country without government, our calamity is heightened by reflecting that we furnish the means by which we suffer.[4]

JOHN A. WIDTSOE

We engage in the election . . . you are to vote for good men, and if you do not do this, *it is a sin*: to vote for wicked men would be a sin. . . . [Curse] the rod of tyranny. . . . Let every man use his liberties according to the Constitution.[5]

In a society like ours, based upon the concept that the individual is sovereign with inalienable, God-given rights, and that individual citizens have formed a government to protect those rights, it is required that a document—a constitution—specify the limits on the powers granted to the government. Just as a government is created to limit the actions of individual citizens, there must be limits placed upon the government as well. In the United States this has been accomplished with the Constitution. The limits were made by defining the areas that the government could operate in, and also where it could place limits on the sovereign individuals who created it.

Each of us has inalienable, God-given rights. Each of us is *equal* in the possession of those rights, and therefore, each of us should be equal in our treatment by law and the government that we created. The right to life, the right to liberty (meaning the ability to choose how we will spend the time of our life and what we will do with our talents to support ourselves and our family), and the right to own and control property are possessed by each individual by virtue of their independent life. To protect these rights, we enter into society and sustain institutions that provide protection against those who stand ready to take advantage of the weak and unaware. But in so doing, we must give up something: we don't get something for nothing. What we give up is a portion of our property through taxes to support the government. We do not, however, give up a portion of our rights when we allow others—our representatives—to decide how our rights will be protected and what portion of our property we will have to relinquish for this protection. Our representatives cannot place limits on our rights or abuse the powers given to them by passing laws contrary to our individual, inalienable rights.

THOMAS JEFFERSON

> Justice is the fundamental law of society; . . . the majority, oppressing an individual, is guilty of a crime; abuses its strength, and by acting on the law of the strongest, breaks up the foundations of society.[6]

Since the creation of a government is such a dangerous proposition, and so many attempts in the past have ended in tyranny or anarchy, people throughout history have looked for better ways to enable such institutions without destroying their inalienable rights in the process. The best system yet devised is that of the United States Constitution, which balances the power of the majority against the inalienable rights of the individual.

JAMES MADISON

> Government is instituted no less for protection of the property, than of the persons, of individuals.[7]

CHAPTER TWO

> But what is government itself but, the greatest of all reflections on human nature? If men were angels, no government would be necessary. . . . The great difficulty lies in this: you must first enable the government to control the governed; and in the next place oblige it to control itself. . . . But experience has taught mankind the necessity of auxiliary precautions.[8]

GEORGE WASHINGTON

> A just estimate of that love of power, and proneness to abuse it, which predominates in the human heart is sufficient to satisfy us of the truth of this position.[9]

The Constitution of the United States of America is a "social contract." It is the contract which the sovereign, individual citizens of society agree to in creating and sustaining the national government. It must be remembered that government is nothing but an institution of force, and can only properly act in a negative fashion to punish crime, and thereby encourage others to obey the law to avoid the punishment. If you do not obey the law, you will lose your life, liberty, or property; through capital punishment, imprisonment, or fines. The Founding Fathers saw all the consequences in the principle and, therefore, fashioned a government built upon the foundation of inalienable rights— also called natural rights—and employed a social contract, which was created by the state governments and then ratified by "the people." To secure the natural rights of the individual citizens, a government was created that was limited in its scope through the social contract that the people, and the government, agreed to. The individual citizens thereby agreed to obey the laws created to regulate their lives *only* in those areas in which they *empowered the government to operate!*

THOMAS PAINE

> A constitution is a thing *antecedent* to a government, and a government is only the creature of a constitution. The constitution of a country is not the act of its government, but of the people constituting a government.[10]

Now when we speak of the proper role of government in society, you know what we mean: those powers which we have agreed to give to our national government to regulate those areas *enumerated* in the social contract. Only a written, social contract that outlines the responsibilities and limitations of government will be honored and sustained by *both the people and the government.* Only this will provide a stable institution that continues to protect the citizen's natural, inalienable rights over time, and only such a government will be sustained by the people and provide a peaceful society.

VIRGINIA CONSTITUTIONAL CONVENTION

That government is no more than a choice among evils, is acknowledged by the most intelligent among mankind, and has been a standing maxim for ages.[11]

EZRA TAFT BENSON

The function of government is to protect life, liberty, and property, and anything more or less than this is usurpation and oppression.[12]

JOHN ADAMS

The moment the idea is admitted into society, that property is not as sacred as the laws of God, and that there is not a force of law and public justice to protect it, anarchy and tyranny commence. If "Thou shalt not covet" and "Thou shalt not steal" were not commandments of Heaven, they must be made inviolable precepts in every society, before it can be civilized or made free.[13]

Some will argue that the society has changed so dramatically since the Constitution was ratified that it no longer applies to an industrial or informational society. Yes, the times have changed since the American Revolution; society is different; technology has changed everything: everything *except* human nature. Was government created to control inanimate things and technology or human nature? Government was created to control, by punishing ill behavior, human nature: man's tendency to take advantage of others. Human nature has not changed since the days of Adam and Eve. However, advances in technology have been made, so man's ability to take advantage of, and do harm to others, through the use of technology has changed.

THOMAS ALLEN

> That, knowing the strong bias of human nature to tyranny and despotism, we have nothing else in view but to provide for posterity against the wanton exercise of power, which cannot otherwise be done than by the formation of a fundamental constitution.[14]

The courts have allowed a transgression of the social contract under the guise that these programs fall under the "General Welfare" or the "Interstate Commerce" clauses. However, there is no way a rational person could read the plain text of the Constitution, understand the basic intent of the Founders to limit the powers of government, and then believe this aforementioned to be true. The entire intent of the Founding Fathers was to create a *limited* government that derived its just powers from the consent of the governed; one that reserved most of the powers to the states individually, as is confirmed by the Ninth Amendment, and to the people individually, as is confirmed by the Tenth Amendment. *We*, the people, have *never* given up our sovereignty through any amendment to the social contract. We have, however, allowed the Supreme Court to interpret the Constitution very loosely to expand the powers of the national government without constitutional amendments. How much sense does it make for the Founding Fathers to empower the judicial branch of the government they were creating, if they wanted to maintain the limits placed upon that government?

A DIVINELY ENDORSED DOCUMENT

Members of The Church of Jesus Christ of Latter-day Saints have more cause to celebrate the founding of the United States of America than any other people. We are taught through inspired documents that the Constitution, and its framers, were raised up by the Lord to perform this important work for the *world* in preparing for the Restoration of the gospel. Indeed, we can say that the Restoration of the gospel began with the restoration of the principles of freedom upon which the Declaration of Independence and the Constitution are based. There could have been no Restoration of the gospel if this country had not been founded upon individual liberty and the freedom of religion.

DOCTRINE AND COVENANTS 101

76 It is my will that they should continue to importune for redress, and redemption, by the hands of those who are placed as rulers and are in authority over you—

77 According to the laws and *constitution of the people, which I have suffered to be established, and should be maintained for the rights and protection of all flesh, according to just and holy principles;*

78 *That every man may act . . . according to the moral agency which I have given unto him,* that *every man may be accountable* for his own sins in the day of judgment.

79 Therefore, it is not right that any man should be in bondage one to another.

80 *And for this purpose have I established the Constitution of this land, by the hands of wise men whom I raised up unto this very purpose,* and redeemed the land by the shedding of blood. (D&C 101:76–80; emphasis added)

DOCTRINE AND COVENANTS 98

4 And now, verily I say unto you concerning the laws of the land.

5 That *law of the land which is constitutional, supporting that principle of freedom in maintaining rights and privileges . . .* is justifiable before me.

6 Therefore, I, the Lord, justify you . . . in befriending that law which *is the constitutional law of the land;*

7 And as pertaining to law of man, *whatsoever is more or less than this, cometh of evil.* (D&C 98:4–7; emphasis added)

CHAPTER TWO

The preface of Doctrine and Covenants section 98 informs us that the revelation was received through the Prophet Joseph Smith in Kirtland, Ohio, on August 6, 1833. With this revelation, the Lord endorsed the US Constitution *as it was at that time.* Since there have been many amendments to the Constitution, and many other changes made to our national government since 1833, we are required to evaluate those changes to determine if they are "more or less than" (D&C 98:7) the original intent of what was given to us by the "hands of wise men whom [the Lord] raised up unto this very purpose" (D&C 101:80). If we, as a people, are looking for political prophets to help shape our political views, we know to look to the Founding Fathers. The purpose of this work is to convey the results of my thirty-five-year investigation into the original intent of the Constitution, which was endorsed by the Lord in 1833, and to compare the *current* understanding and interpretation of the Constitution to the understanding of the Founding Fathers who created it.

There are two other scriptures in the Doctrine and Covenants which we should look at in connection to verse 7 of section 98, mentioned previously, where the Lord uses the expression, "more or less than this cometh of evil."

> For that which is more or less than this cometh of evil, *and shall be attended with cursings and not blessings,* saith the Lord your God. Even so. Amen. (D&C 124:120; emphasis added)

> And whatsoever is more or less than this *is the spirit of that wicked one who was a liar from the beginning.* (D&C 93:25; emphasis added)

These verses should help us to realize the importance of leaving some things alone, for any spirit of improvement upon what the Lord has given us is from the "wicked one" (D&C 93:25) and will be attended with "cursings and not blessings, saith the Lord" (D&C 124:120).

JAMES MADISON

> Do not separate text from historical background. If you do, you
> will have perverted and subverted the Constitution, which can only
> end in a distorted, bastardized form of illegitimate government.[15]

In the spring of 1820, when Joseph Smith Jr. saw the Father and
the Son, he was told to join none of the churches currently available
to him:

> And the Personage who addressed me said that all their creeds were
> an abomination in his sight; that those professors were all cor-
> rupt; that: "they draw near to me with their lips, but their hearts
> are far from me, they teach for doctrines the commandments of
> men, having a form of godliness, but they deny the power thereof."
> (Joseph Smith—History 1:19)

I have always been struck with the last phrase of that verse: "but
they deny the power thereof," and have often contemplated the phrase
in connection with our political beliefs and institutions. Many give
simply lip service to the Constitution, while deep down doubting
the tenets of the freedom it espouses; thereby, "deny[ing] the power
thereof." Each of us wants *our* agency, but doubts if *others* are wise
enough to be allowed to have theirs.

The Wealth of Nations by Adam Smith[16] outlined an economic
framework that dovetails nicely with the political framework created
by the Founding Fathers. The work of the Founding Fathers and Adam
Smith have been woven together in the United States with each supporting the other, and each being necessary for the maintenance of
the other. In *The Wealth of Nations*, Adam Smith illustrates how the
unseen hand of a free economy regulates the whole. That is, as each
individual seeks his or her own "self-interest," he or she regulates the
whole through the dynamic equilibrium created. There is no need for
central control or central planning of the economy, since the control is
ever-present and dynamic, albeit invisible. Those who promote governmental programs to regulate society, business, and/or individuals, do

not believe this and do not trust you as an individual to exercise your agency.

Many in our generation have trouble visualizing how the "unseen hand" successfully works—mainly because we have known little besides government regulation during our lifetimes—but the fact exists that it does work, and it has proven itself for more than a century before we began to allow government in regulating our economy and society. Aren't we "deny[ing] the power" of the free political and economic system we were given by our attempts to regulate, in the name of security, the individual freedom of the Constitution and free enterprise system?

BISHOP JOSEPH L. WIRTHLIN

There has been an apostasy from those divinely given principles of Government which have been transmitted to us by the inspired men who founded this great nation.[17]

ERNEST L. WILKINSON

The sad fact is that nearly every law being passed today is aimed actually at an enlargement of governmental power and a curtailment of individual liberties.[18]

What the Lord, through His inspired agents, originally created for us was a *federal* government composed of state governments with all their sovereign powers, and a national government with very limited and restricted powers designed to accomplish only what the states could not do for themselves. We often think of the government in Washington, D.C., as the *federal* government, but it is only a small part of the system created. It was created to protect the states and the nation from foreign invasion, provide diplomatic intercourse for the states as a whole, provide a uniform set of weights and measures for the nation, and ensure the holding of regular interstate commerce and the interstate waterways between the states, and more. It was determined that all other powers not specifically given to the national government would be held by the state. Even Franklin D. Roosevelt recognized this:

As a matter of fact and law, the governing rights of the States are all of those which have not been surrendered to the National Government by the Constitution . . . such as the conduct of *public utilities*, of *banks*, of *insurance*, of *business*, of *agriculture*, of *education*, of *social welfare*, and of a dozen other important features. *In these, Washington must not be encouraged to interfere.*[19]

This is a strong indication that "whatsoever is more or less than this, cometh of evil" (D&C 98:7).

WILLIAM GODWIN

Since government, even in its best state is an evil, the object principally to be aimed at is that we should have as little of it as the general peace of human society will permit.[20]

The closer the level of government providing the service is to the people, the better operations will be, and the more accountability the people will have.

NOTES

1. Samuel Adams, essay written under the pseudonym "Candidus," in *The Boston Gazette* (October 14, 1771), "A People Who Mean to Be Their Own Governors Must Arm Themselves with the Power which Knowledge Gives," *The Federalist Papers Project*, http://thefederalistpapers.org/founders/samuel-adams/samuel-adams-the-liberties-of-our-country-are-worth-defending.
2. Patrick Henry, June 7, 1788, from "Speech Delivered at the Virginia Convention Debate of the Ratification of the Constitution," *TeachingAmericanHistory.org*, http://teachingamericanhistory.org/library/document/speech-delivered-at-the-virginia-convention-debate-of-the-ratification-of-the-constitution-june-7-1788/.
3. Patrick Henry, in Editorial, *Liberty*, vol. 4, no. 3, Third Quarter, 1909, 18–19.
4. Thomas Paine, *Common Sense*, 1776.
5. John A. Widtsoe, in Conference Report, April 1944.
6. *The Works of Thomas Jefferson*, vol. 11, "To P. S. Dupont de Nemours, April 4, 1816" (New York: Cosimo Classics, 2009), 523.

7. Federalist Papers, no. 54. (All citations of the Federalist Papers in this book were cited from http://www.let.rug.nl/usa/documents/1786-1800/the-federalist-papers/.)

8. Federalist Papers, no. 51.

9. George Washington, Farewell Address, September 19, 1796.

10. Thomas Paine, *Rights of Man*, 1791–92; emphasis added.

11. Patrick Henry, speech delivered at the Virginia Convention, debate of the ratification of the Constitution, June 7, 1788, *TeachingAmericanHistory.org*, http://teachingamericanhistory.org/library/document/speech-delivered-at-the-virginia-convention-debate-of-the-ratification-of-the-constitution-june-7-1788/.

12. Ezra Taft Benson, in Conference Report, April 1968.

13. John Adams, Defence of the Constitutions of Government of the United States of America, ch. 16, doc. 15 (1787).

14. J. E. A. Smith, comp., *The History of Pittsfield, (Berkshire County), Massachusetts, from the Year 1734 to the Year 1800* (Boston: Lee and Shepard, 1869), 353.

15. Steven Fantina, comp., *Of Thee I Speak: A Collection of Patriotic Quotes, Essays, and Speeches* (Integritous Press, 2006), 24.

16. Adam Smith, *An Inquiry into the Nature and Causes of the Wealth of Nations* (London: 1776).

17. Joseph L. Wirthlin, in Conference Report, October 1941, 70.

18. Ernest L. Wilkinson, "The Changing Nature of American Government from a Constitutional Republic to a Welfare State" (Brigham Young University devotional, April 21, 1966).

19. Franklin D. Roosevelt, in Hamilton A. Long, *Your American Yardstick* (Your Heritage Books, 1963), 181; emphasis in original.

20. William Godwin, *An Enquiry Concerning Political Justice*, ed. Mark Philp (London: 1993), 85.

THREE

The Importance of the Constitution

US SUPREME COURT

> The governments are but trustees acting under derived authority and have no power to delegate what is not delegated to them. But the people, as the original fountain might take away what they have delegated and intrust to whom they please. They have the whole title and as absolute proprietors have the right of using or abusing.[1]

> Powers denied are not to be implied; they are to be obtained, if obtained at all, from, and in the manner provided by, those who originally granted the enumerated powers, but who, at the same time, denied powers.[2]

There is definite value to history and the lessons taught therefrom. Historians are more capable of "see[ing] all the consequences in the principle," as James Madison remarked,[3] because they have seen the previous consequences in history. Historians are more capable of seeing through good intentions to the underlining principles. Historians, or any of us that read and value history, can see the danger in the substance when others merely see the appearance of the good intentions and promises. The Constitution seeks to protect from the good

CHAPTER THREE

intentions of well-meaning, well-educated people who cannot, or will not, see the consequences in the principle, but seek to guarantee the inalienable and constitutional rights of the people.

The worth we attribute to every man, the regard in which we hold him, and the sovereignty due him because of his inalienable, God-given rights should take precedence in our minds as Latter-day Saints. It is amusing how "Liberals" (using the contemporary definition of the word) enjoy labeling "Conservatives" as uncompassionate, uncaring, and hateful, while they are often the ones promoting governmental policies while using force to obtain their goals, which usually only benefit a few at the expense of the many. Constitutional Conservatives are actually more caring and compassionate toward others: they don't advocate or sanction the use of force on anyone, or lower their standard of living through governmental redistribution of income laws, for each new "underprivileged" or "disadvantaged" group identified. They allow each individual to have the full right to exercise their life, liberty, and property to benefit themselves and support their families, and Constitutional Conservatives encourage this through the policies they support. Constitutional Conservatives understand, as evidenced throughout history, that each person in society pursuing their own selfish interests counteracts and balances the pursuit of the same by others. The Liberal is unable to accept such "rubbish" because he or she is unable to grasp the concept. The Constitutional Conservative thinks more highly of their fellow citizens and can see how individual charity through private organizations is better able to handle the needs of the poor, the disadvantaged, and the underprivileged. And this approach does not add to the tax burden of fellow citizens, which harms everyone.

Constitutional Conservatives also accept the fact that each individual is unique with distinctive talents and abilities. Each individual then must be free to use those talents in unique ways to support themselves and their families. They accept that they have no just right to restrict the way a person chooses to morally provide for their family. Constitutional Conservatives, therefore, oppose the idea of "central planning" through government that restricts these rights.

THE CONSTITUTION AS A SOCIAL CONTRACT

Next, is the importance of a "social contract." The Constitution of the United States of America is such a document. It is the contract that the sovereign individuals in society agree to in creating and sustaining a government. Since government is nothing but an institution of force, if you do not obey it, you will lose your life, liberty, or property through capital punishment, confinement, or fines: A government's danger must be recognized, and its powers must be limited. The following quote is often inaccurately attributed to George Washington, but the principle is sound:

> Government is *not reason*, it is not eloquence—*it is force*! Like fire, it is a dangerous servant and a fearful master.

PATRICK HENRY

> Guard with jealous attention the public liberty. Suspect every one who approaches that jewel. Unfortunately, nothing will preserve it but downright force. Whenever you give up that force, you are inevitably ruined.[4]

Force is needed to preserve liberty because government is force. This is why the Founding Fathers all accepted as fact what Patrick Henry verbalized so well:

> That government is no more than a choice among evils, is acknowledged by the most intelligent among mankind, and has been a standing maxim for ages.[5]

What our Founding Fathers created for future generations was a government based upon individual liberty, and a national government that was granted specific, limited powers. All powers not given through the social contract were reserved for the states and the individual citizens as specified by the Ninth and Tenth Amendments of the Bill of Rights. We have a constitutional republic whereby we elect representatives to carry out the business of government, but only within limited areas of our lives. We have a written document that specifies what those powers are, and requires an oath by any representative or administrator of the people to honor and defend it as it is written with its original intent. The Constitution even specifies, in Article V, how the powers given to the national government are to be changed through a long and difficult process, designed to be that way, to ensure that the support of the states and the people is had in favor of the change.

With the above being true, how much sense does it make (as we are told repeatedly by politicians and judges) for the people and states to enable one branch of the limited government that they created to define the meaning of the Constitution and expand their powers through the use of the "General Welfare" or "Interstate Commerce" clauses? In other words, how much sense is there to the idea that the Supreme Court is to have the final word on the meaning of the Constitution? Jefferson, Madison, and others did not believe this, but advocated for state nullification of the laws created by the national government. The Virginia and Kentucky Resolutions of 1789,

> were passed by the legislatures of Kentucky and Virginia in response to the Alien and Sedition Acts of 1798 and were authored by Thomas Jefferson and James Madison, respectively. The resolutions argued that the federal government had no authority to exercise power not specifically delegated to it in the Constitution. The Virginia Resolution, authored by Madison, said that by enacting the Alien and Sedition Acts, Congress was exercising "a power not delegated by the Constitution, but on the contrary, expressly and positively forbidden by one of the amendments thereto; a power, which more than any other, ought to produce universal alarm, because it is leveled against that right of freely examining public characters and measures, and of free communication among the people thereon, which has ever been justly deemed, the only effectual guardian of every other right." Madison hoped that other states would register their opposition to the Alien and Sedition Acts as beyond the powers given to Congress. The Kentucky Resolutions,

authored by Jefferson, went further than Madison's Virginia Resolution and asserted that states had the power to nullify unconstitutional federal laws. The Kentucky Resolution declared in part, "The several states who formed that instrument [the Constitution], being sovereign and independent, have the unquestionable right to judge of its infraction; and that a nullification, by those [states], of all unauthorized acts . . . is the rightful remedy."[6]

The states of Connecticut and Wisconsin also exercised this right at a later date regarding other topics. This idea seems to me to be an important check and balance that was placed upon the national government.

PROTECTING INDIVIDUAL RIGHTS

Since the creation of a government was such a dangerous proposition, and so many attempts in the past had ended in tyranny or anarchy, people throughout history have looked for better ways to enable such institutions without destroying their inalienable rights in the process. The best system yet devised is our Constitution, and we as Latter-day Saints know why.

The Founding Fathers saw the consequences in the principle and, therefore, fashioned a government built upon the foundation of inalienable rights—also called natural rights—and they employed a social contract. To secure these natural rights of the individual citizens, they created a government which was limited in its scope through the social contract that the people, states, and national government agreed to. The individuals then agreed to abide by the laws created to regulate their actions *in those areas they empowered the government to operate in only!* The following is a list of the powers specifically given to the national government in Article I of the Constitution:

1. Power to lay and collect taxes, duties, imposts and excises, to pay the debts and provide for the common defense and general welfare of the United States (Section 8)
2. To borrow money on the credit of the United States

3. To regulate commerce with foreign nations, and among the several states

4. To establish an uniform rule of naturalization, and uniform laws on the subject of bankruptcies throughout the United States

5. To coin money, regulate the value thereof, and of foreign coin

6. [To] fix the standard of weights and measures

7. To provide for the punishment of counterfeiting the securities and current coin of the United States

8. To establish post offices and post roads

9. To promote the progress of science and useful arts, *by securing for* limited times to authors and inventors the exclusive right to their respective writings and discoveries

10. To define and punish piracies and felonies committed on the high seas, and offences against the law of nations

11. To declare war, grant letters of marque and reprisal, and make rules concerning captures on land and water

12. To raise and support armies

13. To provide and maintain a navy

14. To provide for calling forth the militia to execute the laws of the union, suppress insurrections and repel invasions

15. To provide for organizing, arming, and disciplining . . . the militia

16. To exercise exclusive legislation . . . over such District . . . as may . . . become the seat of the government of the United States

17. To make all laws which shall be necessary and proper for carrying into execution *the foregoing powers*, and all other powers vested by this Constitution in the government of the United States, or in any department or officer thereof.[7]

JAMES MADISON

The powers delegated by the proposed Constitution to the federal government are few and defined. Those which are to remain in the

State governments are numerous and indefinite. The former will be exercised principally on external objects, as war, peace, negotiation, and foreign commerce; with which last the power of taxation will, for the most part, be connected. The powers reserved to the several States will extend to all the objects which, in the ordinary course of affairs, concern the lives, liberties, and properties of the people, and the internal order, improvement, and prosperity of the State.[8]

The Founding Fathers allowed future generations to change the contract through an intentionally long and deliberative process described in Article V of the Constitution. It has to be a deliberative process if each sovereign individual is to come to a considered decision on the value of the proposed new power given to government and the portion of rights they are to give up in exchange.

JAMES MADISON

The important distinction so well understood in America, between a Constitution established by the people and unalterable by the government, and a law established by the government and alterable by the government, seems to have been little understood and less observed in any other country.[9]

The Constitution requires an oath of office for the president, the members of the House of Representatives, and the Senate. Here is the oath for the president of the United States, as developed by the First Congress in 1789, and later modified after the Civil War:

I do solemnly swear (or affirm) that I will support and defend the Constitution of the United States against all enemies, foreign and domestic; that I will bear true faith and allegiance to the same; that I take this obligation freely, without any mental reservation or purpose of evasion; and that I will well and faithfully discharge the duties of the office on which I am about to enter: So help me God.[10]

The oath for members of the House and Senate is simpler but contains the same spirit:

CHAPTER THREE

I do solemnly swear (or affirm) that I will support the Constitution of the United States.[11]

Since these oaths are required, we must ask ourselves, "To what are they swearing, or affirming, to defend?" A simple answer is to the Constitution, but to what version of the Constitution are they promising to defend? Their own version, or to the original intent of the text as it was written? We have been told for years that we have a "living and breathing" Constitution, by which is meant that the Congress, president, and Supreme Court can make of it anything they want. This, however, is contrary to the intent of a *written* constitution, the spirit of limited government written into the Constitution, and the oath to defend it and bear true faith and allegiance to it. How can anyone, after having read the simple words of the Constitution, and understanding the intent of limited government, believe that Congress, the president, and the Supreme Court—that level of government which the Constitution meant to limit and restrict—can be able to make of it anything beyond its simple meaning *without* a constitutional amendment as required by Article V of the document?

INDIVIDUAL SOVEREIGNTY

Now, when we speak of the proper role of government in society, you know what we mean: the exercising of only those powers which we have agreed to give government through the social contract, as listed above and in the legally ratified amendments to the Constitution. If a governmental power is not to be found in the plainness of the text of the contract, then it is unconstitutional. *We*, each of us individually, are morally able to determine that. If the contract is for everyone in society, then it must be written, as it has been, so that everyone can understand it. We have not given up any of our inalienable rights to judges, bureaucrats, or experts that are not listed in the delegated powers above. Please do not be misled in thinking that you have. If you need an "expert" to explain it to you, then the contract is no good to begin with!

JAMES MADISON

> It will be of little avail to the people . . . if the laws be so volumi-
> nous that they cannot be read, or so incoherent that they cannot
> be understood . . . or undergo such incessant changes that no
> man, who knows what the law is to-day, can guess what it will be
> to-morrow.[12]

What does all this mean? How is one to decide what is proper
and what is not? May I suggest the following: If I cannot come to
your house as an individual, place a gun to your head, and force you
to fund or support my latest harebrained idea, or favorite charity, or
church, then government, by definition, does *not* have this right either.
Yes, it really *is* that simple. Everything else is intended to confuse you
into giving up your rights. Everything else ends in anarchy, or tyranny. Only a written, social contract that outlines the responsibilities
and limitations of government, and a government which adheres to
these limitations, can be sustained by the people and remain a stable
government that retains the rights of the people for their children.
Government cannot protect us from every potential danger, and it's
not empowered by the social contract to due so. It was created to protect our rights; it is when we expect more than this of it that we start
going astray.

BENJAMIN FRANKLIN

> Those who would give up essential Liberty, to purchase a little
> temporary safety, deserve neither Liberty nor Safety.[13]

Even Franklin D. Roosevelt understood the limitations placed on
the national government by the people through the Constitution: "As
a matter of fact and law, the governing rights of the States are all of
those which have not been surrendered to the National Government
by the Constitution . . . such as the conduct of *public utilities*, of *banks*,
of *insurance*, of *business*, of *agriculture*, of *education*, of *social welfare*,
and of a dozen other important features. *In these, Washington must not
be encouraged to interfere.*"[14]

CHAPTER THREE

If the American people *really* wanted any of the "New Deal" or "Great Society" programs, the only way they could have them, *and honor the social contract* (the Constitution), would be to amend the document through the process outlined within it. If the majority of the people saw value in supporting these programs, we would have them constitutionally. As the document reads today, there is nothing contained therein that empowers NASA, HUD, EPA, OSHA, EEOC, DOE, FAA, FDA, FCC, BLM, and more. The courts have allowed this transgression of the social contract under the guise that it falls under the "General Welfare" clause, the "Interstate Commerce" clause, or the Civil War Amendments. However, there is no way a rational person could read the plainness of the document, while understanding the basic intent of limiting the powers of government, and believe this. The entire intent of the Founding Fathers was to create a *limited* government that derived its just powers from the consent of the governed; one that reserved most of the powers for the states individually, and to the people individually as the Ninth and Tenth Amendments reiterate.

We, the people, have *never* given up our sovereignty through any amendment to the social contract. *We* still possess the natural right to overthrow our government when it becomes too oppressive. The Declaration of Independence reads:

> We hold these truths to be self-evident, that all men are created equal, that they are endowed by their Creator with certain unalienable Rights, that among these are Life, Liberty and the pursuit of Happiness. That to secure these rights, Governments are instituted among Men, deriving their just powers from the consent of the governed. That whenever any Form of Government becomes destructive of these ends, it is the Right of the People to alter or to abolish it, and to institute new Government, laying its foundation on such principles and organizing its powers in such form, as to them shall seem most likely to effect their Safety and Happiness. Prudence, indeed, will dictate that Governments long established should not be changed for light and transient causes;

and accordingly all experience hath shown that mankind are more disposed to suffer, while evils are sufferable, than to right themselves by abolishing the forms to which they are accustomed. *But when a long train of abuses and usurpations, pursuing invariably the same object evinces [shows plainly] a design to reduce them under absolute Despotism, it is their right, it is their duty, to throw off such Government, and to provide new Guards for their future security.*[15]

This is the core of what it is to be an American! You are the sovereign under God because He has made you that way. You have the rights from Him; and *you* created and empowered government through those inalienable rights. It is not the other way around. Government exists because *you* have rights; you do not have rights because government has given them to you. Government is your servant, not your master. *You* created it to protect the rights that each one of us have. It was created to treat all its citizens, who empower it, equally. Its burdens were to be born equally by each of the citizens that were equally protected by it.

JOHN MARSHALL

The particular phraseology of the Constitution of the United States confirms and strengthens the principle, supposed to be essential to all written Constitutions, that a law repugnant to the Constitution is void, and that courts, as well as other departments, are bound by that instrument.[16]

JAMES MADISON

The important distinction so well understood in America, between a Constitution established by the people and unalterable by the government, and a law established by the government and alterable by the government, seems to have been little understood and less observed in any other country.[17]

A free society can only exist as long as both the people and the government sustain, support, and defend the social contract. It cannot be long sustained if either party usurps power or authority that is not clearly defined in the social contract. Even though government has the physical power to deprive a person of life, liberty, or property if he or she fails to support it—assuming immoral government agents (fellow citizens) can be found to do such a thing—there is still the states, the Second Amendment, and the state militias as a final legal recourse.

LOUIS C. BRANDEIS

> Crime is contagious. If the government becomes a lawbreaker, it breeds contempt for law.[18]

Our Founding Fathers took their individual sovereignty seriously; it was not a passing fancy for them. Their sovereignty was the cornerstone of life; since life without liberty, and liberty without the right to own and control property, has no meaning: individuals become puppets to be controlled by others, with no capability to act on their own, which is the fundamental principle of learning. If you think about it, the rights of life, liberty, and property have no meaning without the ability to defend them; so, even though we think about them as being three separate rights, they are really just one right to protect three things: we are justified by God in using force, up to and including lethal force, to protect our life, the life of others, our liberty, and our property. Because this is difficult for most of us, we have created government to protect these rights for us, but look carefully at the wording of the following scriptures in Doctrine and Covenants 134:

> 1 We believe that governments were instituted of God for the benefit of man; and that he holds men accountable for their acts in relation to them, both in making laws and administering them, for the good and safety of society.
>
> 2 We believe that no government can exist in peace, except such laws are framed and held inviolate as will secure to each individual the free exercise of conscience, the right and control of property, and the protection of life.

3 We believe that all governments necessarily require civil officers and magistrates to enforce the laws of the same; and that such as will administer the law in equity and justice should be sought for and upheld by the voice of the people if a republic, or the will of the sovereign.

4 We believe that religion is instituted of God; and that men are amenable to him, and to him only, for the exercise of it, unless their religious opinions prompt them to infringe upon the rights and liberties of others; but we do not believe that human law has a right to interfere in prescribing rules of worship to bind the consciences of men, nor dictate forms for public or private devotion; that the civil magistrate should restrain crime, but never control conscience; should punish guilt, but never suppress the freedom of the soul.

5 We believe that all men are bound to sustain and uphold the respective governments in which they reside, *while protected in their inherent and inalienable rights by the laws of such governments*; and that sedition and rebellion are unbecoming every citizen *thus protected*, and should be punished accordingly; and that all governments have a right to enact such laws as in their own judgments are best calculated to secure the public interest; at the same time, however, holding sacred the freedom of conscience. (D&C 134:1–5)

While we're on this subject, let's discuss another scripture often quoted by Church members: "We believe in being subject to kings, presidents, rulers, and magistrates, in obeying, honoring, and sustaining the law" (Articles of Faith 1:12). Now you can see that there are limits to "obeying, honoring, and sustaining the law"; this is only true "while protected in [our] inherent and inalienable rights by the laws of such governments" (D&C 134:5). This is why we can honor the Founding Fathers for *not* obeying the law of their time and for overthrowing the British crown to establish our free country with constitutional protections.

CHAPTER THREE

THE IMPORTANCE OF LIBERTY

There can be no personal growth without liberty. There is no purpose to life without liberty. Our moral responsibility to others is ours individually, not collectively. No collectivist society (socialist, communist, utopian) has long survived—ask any historian. Constitutionalists believe in the inherent goodness and charity of the vast majority of individuals, and there will *always* be those who attempt to operate outside of moral laws. Constitutionalists respect others enough to realize that, given unrestrained opportunity, each individual will harvest the bounties of life and be willing to voluntarily share them with others through private charitable organizations, which are immediately accountable to the people who support them, so that, no ineffective or costly charitable organization will long survive.

Just as there is no meaning to life without liberty, there is no meaning to liberty without property, no meaning property without the right to control it, and no meaning to the right to control property without the right to its defense, and the right to buy and sell in a free market society. All of these issues must be elements of the social contract of any free society if it is to long exist. If any one of the parts falls, just like a line of dominoes, they all fall.

I am a constitutionalist: I wish to conserve the virtues, principles, and values our forefathers died to preserve, and established in the US Constitution. I love the Founding Fathers and I revere their names. Long live those who struggle to preserve the social contract founded upon these virtues and principles that hold us together as a unified nation of separate states. Long live those who courageously stand alone in the streets against any form of oppression. Long live those who suffer, bleed, and die in the defense of our natural rights.

THOMAS JEFFERSON

I have sworn upon the altar of god eternal hostility against every form of tyranny over the mind of man.[19]

WILLIAM PITT

| Necessity . . . is the argument of tyrants; it is the creed of slaves.[20]

NOTES

1. US Supreme Court in Luther vs. Borden, 48 US 1, 12 LED 581.
2. *Cases Argued and Decided in the Supreme Court of the United States* bk. 64 (Rochester, New York: The Lawyers Co-operative Publishing Company, 1920), 644.
3. US Constitution, Amend. I, doc. 43.
4. Patrick Henry, in Jonathan Elliot, *The Debates in the Several State Conventions on the Adoption of the Federal Constitution as Recommended by the General Convention at Philadelphia in 1787*, vol. 3 (New York: Burt Franklin, 1888), 45.
5. Ibid.; 137.
6. "Virginia and Kentucky Resolutions (1798)," *Bill of Rights Institute*, http://billofrightsinstitute.org/founding-documents/primary-source-documents/virginia-and-kentucky-resolutions/.
7. US Constitution, Art. I, Sec. 8; emphasis added.
8. Federalist Papers, no. 45.
9. Federalist Papers, no. 53.
10. Oath of Office; see "Oath of Office," *United States Senate*, https://www.senate.gov/artandhistory/history/common/briefing/Oath_Office.htm.
11. Ibid.
12. Federalist Papers, no. 62.
13. Benjamin Franklin, in *Votes and Proceedings of the House of Representatives*, 1755–56 (Philadelphia, 1756), 19–21.
14. Franklin D. Roosevelt, in Hamilton A. Long, *Your American Yardstick* (Your Heritage Books, 1963), 181; emphasis in original.
15. Declaration of Independence; emphasis added.
16. Chief Justice Marshall, opinion, in Marbury vs. Madison, 1803.
17. Federalist Papers, no. 53.
18. Justice Louis D. Brandeis, opinion, in Olmstead vs. United States, 1928.
19. Thomas Jefferson to Benjamin Rush, September 23, 1800, in *The Papers of Thomas Jefferson* (Princeton: Princeton University Press, 1950), 32:168.
20. William Pitt, in speech in the House of Commons, November 8, 1783.

FOUR

Presidents of the Church on the US Constitution, Government, and Agency

The presidents of the Church following Joseph Smith Jr. and Brigham Young have expressed their views on the Constitution, the US Government, and agency. To preface their comments, let's start with a quote by former Brigham Young University president Ernest L. Wilkinson:

> The Prophet Joseph once said that it was the duty of the prophets to advise us on temporal as well as spiritual matters and that the two are inseparably connected. President John Taylor also advised that the elders of Israel should ". . . understand that they have something to do with the world politically as well as religiously, that it is as much their duty to study correct political principles as well as religious." Besides the preaching of the Gospel, we have another mission, namely, the perpetuation of the free agency of man and the maintenance of liberty, freedom, and the rights of man. I know that there are some who try to differentiate between advice given by our leaders on religious matters and advice which they allege pertains to political matters, claiming that we do not need to follow the Prophet when he advises us on political matters. Of course we don't; neither are we required to follow him on spiritual matters; neither are we required to keep the Ten Commandments, for the

Lord himself has given us our free agency. But if we are faithful members of the Church, and if we want the blessings of liberty for ourselves and our posterity, we are under the same moral obligation to follow his advice on political as on religious matters.[1]

JOSEPH SMITH JR.

The Constitution of the United States is a glorious standard; it is founded in the wisdom of God. It is a heavenly banner; it is to all those who are privileged with the sweets of liberty, like the cooling shades and refreshing waters of a great rock in a thirsty and weary land. It is like a great tree under whose branches men from every clime can be shielded from the burning rays of the sun.[2]

JOHN TAYLOR

When the people shall have torn to shreds the Constitution of the United States, the elders of Israel will be found holding it up to the nations of the earth, and proclaiming liberty and equal rights to all men, and extending the hand of fellowship to the oppressed of all nations.[3]

EZRA TAFT BENSON, QUOTING JOSEPH SMITH

Even this Nation will be on the very verge of crumbling to pieces and tumbling to the ground, and when the constitution is upon the brink of ruin, this people will be the staff upon which the nation shall lean, and they shall bear the Constitution away from the very verge of destruction.[4]

BRIGHAM YOUNG

The signers of the Declaration of Independence and the framers of the Constitution were inspired from on high to do that work.[5]

JOHN TAYLOR

It was by and through the power of God, that the fathers of this country framed the Declaration of Independence, and also that great palladium of human rights, the Constitution of the United States.[6]

WILFORD WOODRUFF

Those men who laid the foundation of this American government and signed the Declaration of Independence were the best spirits the God of heaven could find on the face of the earth. They were choice spirits, not wicked men. General Washington and all the men that labored for the purpose were inspired of the Lord.[7]

LORENZO SNOW

We trace the hand of the Almighty in framing the constitution of our land, and believe that the Lord raised up men purposely for the accomplishment of this object, raised them up and inspired them to frame the Constitution of the United States.[8]

JOSEPH F. SMITH

I hope with all my soul that the members of the Church of Jesus Christ of Latter-day Saints will be loyal in their very hearts and souls, to the principles of the Constitution of our country. From them we have derived the liberty that we enjoy. They have been the means of guaranteeing to the foreigner that has come within our gates, and to the native born, and to all the citizens of this country, the freedom and liberty that we possess. We cannot go back upon such principles as these.[9]

HEBER J. GRANT

From my childhood days I have understood that we believe absolutely that the Constitution of our country was an inspired instrument, and that God directed those who created it and those who defended the independence of this nation. In other words, that He fought with Washington and others in the Revolutionary War.[10]

GEORGE ALBERT SMITH

The Lord himself said that he raised up the very men who framed the Constitution of the United States and directed that the membership of this Church should pray for and sustain those who represented the Constitution of this land. . . . You know, and I know, that the Ten Commandments contain the will of our Heavenly Father, and I am grateful, not only for the civil laws but also for the laws God has given us. I feel bound to conform my life to the teachings of the Ten Commandments. I feel equally bound to sustain the Constitution of the United States which came from the same source as the Ten Commandments. Unless the people of this great nation can realize these things and repent, they may forfeit the liberty that they now enjoy, and the blessings that are so multiplied among us.[11]

DAVID O. MCKAY

Next to being one in worshiping God, there is nothing in this world upon which this Church should be more united than in upholding and defending the Constitution of the United States.[12]

JOSEPH FIELDING SMITH

Our government came into existence through divine guidance. The inspiration of the Lord rested upon the patriots who established it, and inspired them through the dark days of their struggle for independence and through the critical period which followed that struggle when they framed our glorious Constitution which guarantees to all the self-evident truth proclaimed in the Declaration of Independence, "that all men are created equal: that they are endowed by their Creator with certain inalienable rights: that among these are life, liberty, and the pursuit of happiness."[13]

SPENCER W. KIMBALL

This restoration was preceded by a long period of preparation. The Pilgrims and other Europeans were inspired to find this American

CHAPTER FOUR

haven of refuge and thus people this land with honest and God-fearing citizens. Washington and his fellows were inspired to revolt from England and bring political liberty to this land, along with the more valuable treasure of religious liberty so that the soil might be prepared for the seed of the truth when it should again be sown.[14]

EZRA TAFT BENSON

Yes, the early leaders and the people generally of this great nation recognized the necessity for spiritual support if the nation was to endure. They gave humble expression to this conviction in the inscription, "In God We Trust" found on the coins of the land. The holy Sabbath was a day of rest and worship. Religious devotion in the home was a common practice. Family prayer, reading of the holy scriptures, and the singing of hymns were an everyday occurrence. There is every evidence that "our fathers looked to God for their direction." In framing that great document which Gladstone declared "the most wonderful work ever struck off at a given time by the brain and purpose of man," our early leaders called upon a kind Providence. Later the product of the constitutional convention was referred to as our God-inspired Constitution. They had incorporated within its sacred paragraphs eternal principles supported by the holy scriptures with which they were familiar. It was established "for the rights and protection of all flesh according to just and holy principles" (D&C 101:80).[15]

HOWARD W. HUNTER

Christianity in its fulness and truth has been restored to the earth by direct revelation. The restoration of the Gospel of Jesus Christ is the most significant fact since the resurrection of Jesus Christ. What was restored? In a very real sense, the true Law of the Harvest was restored—the law of justice, the law of mercy, the law of love. It was restored in a free country under the influence of a God-inspired Constitution which created a climate of freedom, opportunity and prosperity. The basic virtues of thrift, self-reliance, independence, enterprise, diligence, integrity, morality, faith in God and in His Son, Jesus Christ, were the principles upon which this, the greatest nation in the world, has been built. We must not sell this priceless, divine heritage which was largely paid for by the blood of patriots and prophets for a mess of pottage, for a counterfeit, a false doctrine parading under the cloak of love and compassion, of humanitarianism, even of Christianity.[16]

GORDON B. HINCKLEY

Both the Declaration of Independence and the Constitution of the United States were brought forth under the inspiration of God to establish and maintain the freedom of the people of this nation. I said it, and I believe it to be true. There is a miracle in its establishment that cannot be explained in any other way.[17]

THOMAS S. MONSON

Let us pause and reflect upon the many blessings we as Americans have received from our Constitution and the debt of gratitude we owe those heroic signers. As we do so, we might also recognize that freedom is not free. Sacrifice has been required to protect and to preserve the very freedoms we cherish.[18]

DEFENDING THE CONSTITUTION

JOSEPH FIELDING SMITH, QUOTING JOSEPH SMITH

The Constitution of the United States is a glorious standard. It is founded in the wisdom of God. It is a heavenly banner: it is to all those who are privileged with the sweets of its liberty, like the cooling shades and refreshing waters of a great rock in a thirsty and weary land. It is like a great tree under whose branches men from every clime can be shielded from the burning rays of the sun. . . . It is one of the first principles of my life and one that I have cultivated from my childhood, having been taught it by my father, to allow everyone the liberty of conscience. I am the greatest advocate of the Constitution of the United States there is on earth. In my feelings I am always ready to die for the protection of the weak and the oppressed in their just rights.[19]

I must not take more time but to add this: The statement has been made that the Prophet said the time would come when this Constitution would hang as by a thread, and this is true. There has been some confusion, however, as to just what he said following this. I think that Elder Orson Hyde has given us a correct interpretation wherein he says that the Prophet said the Constitution would be in danger. Said Orson Hyde: I believe he said something like this—that the time would come when the Constitution and the country would be in danger of an overthrow; and said he: "If the Constitution be saved at all, it will be by the Elders of this Church." I believe this is about the language, as nearly as I can recollect it.[20] Now I tell you it is time the people of the United States were waking up with the understanding that if they don't save the Constitution from the dangers that threaten it, we will have a change of government.[21]

Joseph Smith became rather frustrated by the treatment of the Latter-day Saints during his time and ultimately decided to run for president of the United States. Consequently, he wrote and published *General Smith's Views of the Powers and Policy of the Government of the United States* in 1844.[22] The quotations below are taken from that document. In it, he praises the administrations of George Washington, John Adams, Thomas Jefferson, James Madison, James Monroe, John Quincy Adams, and Andrew Jackson, but then adds "General Jackson's administration may be denominated the acme of American glory, liberty, and prosperity; for the national debt . . . was paid up in his golden day. . . . At the age, then, of sixty years, our blooming republic began to decline."

He adds "'Since the fathers have fallen asleep,' wicked and designing men have unrobed the government of its glory, and the people, if not in dust and ashes, or in sack cloth, have to lament in poverty, her departed greatness, while demagogues build fires in the north and the south, east and west, to keep up their spirits *till it is better times*; but year after year has left the people to *hope* till the very name of *Congress* or *State Legislature* is as horrible to the sensitive friend of his country, as the house of 'Bluebeard' is to children; or 'Crockford's' Hell of London, to meek men."[23]

The Prophet Joseph indicates elsewhere in the document that the acts of legislative bodies are not always appropriate. He says, "Nor am I less surprised at the *stretches of power*, or *restrictions of right*, which too often appear as acts of legislators, to pave the way to some favorite political scheme, as destitute of intrinsic merit, as a wolf's heart is of the milk of human kindness."[24]

Joseph Smith believed that the purpose of government was to safeguard the rights of the citizens, and that their support of government was conditional upon this fact. He continues, "General Jackson, upon his ascension to the great chair of the chief magistracy, said, 'As long as our government is administered for the good of the people, and is regulated by their will; as long as it secures to us the rights of person and property, liberty of conscience, and of the press, it will be worth defending; and so long as it is worth defending, a patriotic militia will cover it with an impenetrable *aegis*'" [originally a mythological term *meaning* "protective shield" or "defensive armor"].[25]

He also expressed his belief that the powers of government had already started to exceed the limitations of the Constitution. Quoting President William Henry Harrison, he says, "Knowing the tendency of power to increase itself, . . . I sincerely believe that the tendency of measures and of men's opinions, for some years past, has been in that direction. . . . I have heretofore given, of my determination to arrest the progress of that tendency." Joseph then added, "This good man died before he had the opportunity of applying one balm to ease the pain of our groaning country. . . . No honest man can doubt for a moment, but the glory of American liberty, is on the wane."[26]

CHAPTER FOUR

JOHN TAYLOR

> We do not wish to place ourselves in a state of antagonism, nor to act defiantly, towards this government. We will fulfil the letter, so far as practicable, of that unjust, inhuman, oppressive and unconstitutional law, so far as . . . we can without violating principle; but we cannot sacrifice every principle of human right at the behest of corrupt, unreasoning and unprincipled men; we cannot violate the highest and noblest principles of human nature and make pariahs and outcasts of high-minded, virtuous and honorable women, nor sacrifice at the shrine of popular clamor the highest and noblest principles of humanity!
>
> We shall abide all constitutional law, as we always have done; but while we are Godfearing and law-abiding, and respect all honorable men and officers, we are no craven serfs, and have not learned to lick the feet of oppressors, nor to bow in base submission to unreasoning clamor. We will contend, inch by inch, legally and constitutionally, for our rights as American citizens, and for the universal rights of universal man. We stand proudly erect in the consciousness of our rights as American citizens, and plant ourselves firmly on the sacred guarantees of the Constitution; and that instrument, while it defines the powers and privileges of the President, Congress and the judiciary, also directly provides that "the powers not delegated to the United States by the Constitution, nor prohibited by it to the States, are reserved to the States respectively or to the people."[27]

These statements are really nothing more than the restatement of the sentiments of our Declaration of Independence:

> We hold these truths to be self-evident, that all men are created equal, that they are endowed by their Creator with certain unalienable Rights, that among these are Life, Liberty and the pursuit of Happiness. That to secure these rights, Governments are instituted among Men, deriving their just powers from the consent

of the governed. That whenever *any Form* of Government becomes destructive of these ends, it is the Right of the People to alter or to abolish it, and to institute new Government, . . . when a long train of abuses and usurpations, pursuing invariably the same Object evinces a design to reduce them under absolute Despotism, it is their *right*, it is their *duty*, to throw off *such Government*, and to provide new Guards for their future security.[28]

As an interesting sidebar, the Prophet Joseph Smith made some interesting recommendations for the United States in *General Smith's Views of the Powers and Policy of the Government of the United States*, including:

1. The abolition of slavery by the year 1850 by purchasing the slaves from their owners—recognizing the right of property.
2. Prison confinement or death for murder only—"larceny, burglary, or any felony" to be punished by "work upon roads, public works, or any place where the culprit can be taught more wisdom and more virtue; and become more enlightened"—equivalent to the limitation of the Law of Moses eye for an eye.
3. Economic protection through judicious tariffs—which were the primary revenue source allowed by the Constitution for the national government.
4. The reduction of the size of Congress by "at least one half" resulting in "two Senators from a state and two members to a million of population."
5. "Curtail[ing] the offices of government in pay, number and power."
6. Abolishing the military practice of "trying men by court martial for desertion"—he believed it would be sufficient punishment to instruct him "that his country will never trust him again" and that "he has forfeited his honor."
7. "More economy in the national and state governments, would make less taxes among the people."
8. The creation of a national bank "where the capital stock [is] held by the nation," and "whose officers [are] elected yearly by the people," and

the profit of the bank to "be applied to the national revenue" to save taxes—compare this to the unconstitutional, unaccountable Federal Reserve System we have today.

9.   The repeal of the requirement "for the governor of a state to [have to] make [a] demand of the president for troops, in case of invasion or rebellion."

10. "Send every lawyer as soon as he repents . . . to preach the gospel to the destitute."[29]

Joseph Smith made two other interesting comments. One is "Open the hearts of all people, to behold and enjoy freedom, unadulterated freedom."[30] This leads me to believe that he was saying what I expressed above regarding "teaching for doctrines the commandments of men" (establishing for law the philosophies of men), "having a form of godliness" (appearing to be true liberty), but denying the power thereof. His other comment is, "Wherefore, were I president of the United States, by the voice of a virtuous people, I would honor the old paths of the venerated fathers of freedom; I would walk in the tracks of the illustrious patriots who carried the ark of the government upon their shoulders with an eye single to the glory of the people."[31] This is what I think we should have the courage to do also: look for the answers to our current problems in the past by accepting the original intent of the Constitution and not "deny[ing] the power thereof" (see 2 Timothy 3:5). For this reason, I began my thirty-five-year search into the writings of the Founding Fathers to understand the original intent of their creation.

PROTECTING RELIGIOUS FREEDOM

Most of Brigham Young's comments on the subject of government and the Constitution concern separating, in our minds, the virtue and honor of the Constitution given to us by our Heavenly Father, and the administration of the laws of the government that it created. Brigham Young ever spoke out in favor of the Constitution; his comments on the administrators of government weren't so supportive. He said,

I do not lift my voice against the great and glorious Government guaranteed to every citizen by our Constitution, but against those corrupt administrators who trample the Constitution and just laws under their feet.[32]

And if this was true *then*, how much more so *now*? Abraham Lincoln made a similar, yet more forceful statement on this subject that bears repeating:

We must prevent each of these things being done by either congresses or courts. The people of these United States are the rightful masters of both congresses and courts, not to overthrow the Constitution, but to overthrow the men who pervert the Constitution.[33]

Brigham Young made the following comment supporting the premise of chapter 2 regarding the Constitution as a social contract, and the importance of it being honored by the government itself, as well as by the people.

It is a pretty bold stand for this people to take, to say that they will not be controlled by the corrupt administrators of our General Government. We will be controlled by them, if they will be controlled by the Constitution and laws; but they will not. Many of them do not care any more about the Constitution and the laws that they make than they do about the laws of another nation. That class trample the rights of the people under their feet, while there are many who would like to honor them. All we have ever asked for is our constitutional rights. We wish the laws of our Government honored, and we have ever honored them; but they are trampled under foot by administrators.[34]

Not only are they currently "trampled under foot by administrators," but by politicians and judges as well.

CHAPTER FOUR

When we begin to evaluate the changes to the Constitution, you will be asked to determine if those changes are of a trifling nature, or if they are anything "more or less than" what the Lord endorsed.

Now we come to the words of Joseph Smith, given to us by Brigham Young. These very words started my search into the original intent of the Constitution.

BRIGHAM YOUNG, QUOTING JOSEPH SMITH

How long will it be before the words of the prophet Joseph will be fulfilled? He said *if the Constitution of the United States were saved at all* it must be done by this people. It will not be many years before these words come to pass.[35]

When the Constitution of the United States hangs, as it were, upon a single thread, they will have to call for the "Mormon" Elders to save it from utter destruction; and they will step forth and do it.[36]

EZRA TAFT BENSON, QUOTING JOSEPH SMITH

Even this nation will be on the very verge of crumbling to pieces and tumbling to the ground and, when the Constitution is upon the brink of ruin, this people will be the staff upon which the nation shall lean, and they shall bear the Constitution away from the very verge of destruction.[37]

ORSON HYDE, QUOTING JOSEPH SMITH

It is said that Brother Joseph in his lifetime declared that the Elders of this Church should step forth at a particular time when the Constitution should be in danger, and rescue it, and save it. This may be so; but I do not recollect that he said exactly so. I believe he said something like this—that the time would come when the Constitution and the country would be in danger of an overthrow; and said he, *if* the Constitution be saved at all, it will be by the Elders of this Church. I believe this is about the language, as nearly as I can recollect it.[38]

President Brigham Young said that the Prophet Joseph Smith declared,

> The time will come when the destiny of the nation will hang by a single thread. At that critical juncture, this people will step forth and save it from the threatened destruction.[39]

JAMES BURGESS

> In the month of May 1843. Several miles east of Nauvoo. The Nauvoo Legion was on parade and review. At the close of which Joseph Smith made some remarks upon our condition as a people and upon our future prospects contrasting our present condition with our past trials and persecutions by the hands of our enemies. Also upon the constitution and government of the United States stating that the time would come when the Constitution and Government would hang by a *brittle* thread and would be ready to fall into other hands but this people the Latter-day Saints will step forth and save it. General Scott and part of his staff on the American Army was present on the occasion. I James Burgess was present and testify to the above.[40]

This is the political motto of the Church as written by Joseph Smith Jr.:

> The Constitution of our country *formed by the Fathers of Liberty*; peace and good order in society; love to God, and good will to man. All good and wholesome laws; virtue and truth above all things, and Aristarchy [fn: "A body of good men at the head of government"], live for ever! but woe to tyrants, mobs, aristocracy, anarchy, and toryism, and all those who invent or seek out unrighteous and vexatious law suits, under the pretext and color of law, or office, either religious or political. . . . And let all the people say Amen! that the blood of the fathers may not cry from the ground against us. Sacred is the memory of that blood which bought for us our liberty.[41]

Joseph also said that the world is governed too much!

As the "*world is governed too much*" and as there is not a nation or dynasty, now occupying the earth, which acknowledges Almighty God as their law giver, and as "crowns won by blood, by blood must be maintained," I go emphatically, virtuously, and humanely, for a THEODEMOCRACY, where God and the people hold the power to conduct the affairs of men in righteousness. And where liberty, free trade, and sailor's rights, and the protection of life and property shall be maintained inviolate, for the benefit of ALL.[42]

THE DUTY OF LATTER-DAY SAINTS

In January 1987, the First Presidency restated the Church's view that the Constitution is an inspired document, and encouraged Americans to take advantage of the bicentennial celebration:

We encourage Latter-day Saints throughout the nation to familiarize themselves with the Constitution. They should focus attention on it by reading and studying it. They should ponder the blessings that come through it. They should recommit themselves to its principles and be prepared to defend it and the freedom it provides.[43]

President Benson delivered two landmark speeches on the US Constitution during his presidency, one at a BYU devotional on September 16, 1986,[43] and the other at general conference on October 3, 1987.[44] Similar in content, the talks were in observance of the bicentennial of the US Constitution, which was signed September 1787. On both occasions, the prophet warned:

We are fast approaching that moment prophesied by Joseph Smith when he said: "Even this nation will be on the very verge of crumbling to pieces and tumbling to the ground, and when the Constitution is upon the brink of ruin, this people will be the staff upon which the nation shall lean, and they shall bear the Constitution away from the very verge of destruction."[45]

President Benson listed four things that citizens must do to befriend and safeguard the Constitution:

1. We must be righteous and moral.
2. We must learn the principles of the Constitution and then abide by its precepts.
3. We must become involved in civic affairs.
4. We must make our influence felt by our vote, our letters, and our advice.[46]

Ezra Taft Benson, speaking at BYU, said understanding the significance of the Constitution requires understanding *basic eternal principles* that have their beginning in the pre-mortal councils of heaven.

"The first basic principle is agency. . . . The second basic principle concerns the function and proper role of government. . . . The third important principle pertains to the source of basic human rights. . . . The fourth basic principle we must understand is that people are superior to the governments they form. . . . The fifth and final principle . . . is that governments should have only limited powers."[47] Then, in his conference talk, the prophet declared, "I reverence the Constitution of the United States as a sacred document. To me its words are akin to the revelations of God, for God has placed His stamp of approval upon it."[48]

And now we come to my personal favorite quotation by President David O. McKay:

Next to being one in worshiping God, there is nothing in this world upon which this Church should be more united than in upholding and defending the Constitution of the United States.[49]

If Zion is defined as a people of "one heart and one mind" (Moses 7:18), our political ideology, as well as our religious beliefs, should be the same for all members of the Church. There should not need to be much discussion on this, since the Lord has declared it.

Since almost four generations have been raised in the United States since the fundamental changes mentioned in this book were made to our constitutional system, and since these changes have been accepted by the people with little discussion, and taught as if they were part of the original document given to us and endorsed by Heavenly Father, I thought this work might be necessary to inform the "Mormon" elders of the original intent and meaning of the Constitution, if "this people the Latter-day Saints will step forth and save it,"[50] "if the Constitution be saved at all."[51]

MELVIN J. BALLARD

I say to you that every institution or man that takes away from the people their free agency and their liberty is not of God. I care not how beneficial its purposes may be, if it takes away from man his liberty and free agency, it is working in harmony with that rejected and fallen son of God.[52]

EZRA TAFT BENSON

Sometimes the Lord hopefully waits on his children to act on their own, and when they do not, they lose the greater prize, and the Lord will either drop the entire matter and let them suffer the consequences or else He will have to spell it out in greater detail. Usually, I fear, the more He has to spell it out, the smaller is our reward.[53]

It was the struggle over free agency that divided us before we came here; it may well be the struggle over the same principle which will deceive and divide us again.[54]

ALBERT E. BOWEN

There is no soul-growth in any act done under compulsion. It is an immutable law of life that mental or spiritual growth comes only out of self-effort.[55]

DAVID O. MCKAY

There cannot be happiness without free agency. If the soul feels circumscribed, harassed, or enslaved by something or somebody, there cannot be true progress. That is why some of the nations today are wrong and someday in the future will have to change their policy. God intends men to be free.[56]

The *third* cornerstone [of Zion's inhabitants] is a realization that the first and most essential thing in man's progress is freedom—*free agency.* Man can choose the highest good, or choose the lowest good and fall short of what he was intended to be.[57]

Free agency is the impelling force of the soul's progress.[58]

HENRY D. MOYLE

There isn't a social order on earth today but what if we were to follow it long enough and far enough would rob us of our free agency.[59]

Are we going to sacrifice our chances to retain our own free agency for anything that the world has to offer? All we have to do is just to examine any movement that may be brought into our midst whether it be social or political or what not, and if it has the earmarks of an attempt to deprive us in the slightest respect of our free agency, we should avoid it as we would avoid immorality or anything else that is vicious. I am sure that free agency is as necessary for our eternal salvation as is our virtue. And just as we guard our virtue with our lives, so should we guard our free agency. It has been my experience . . . that wherever I permit anyone to perform any of the functions which the Lord expected I should perform for myself, that to the extent I do this, I become that other man's slave.[60]

MARION G. ROMNEY

The preservation of free agency is more important than the preservation of life itself.[61]

We have a classic example of the loss of economic freedom by the misuse of free agency in the Book of Genesis. The Egyptians, instead of exercising their agency to provide for themselves against a day of need, depended upon the government. As a result, when the famine came they were forced to purchase food from the government. First they used their money. When that was gone, they gave their livestock, then their lands; and finally they were compelled to sell themselves into [economic] slavery, that they might eat. We ourselves have gone a long way down this road during the last century. My counsel is that we beware of the doctrine that encourages us to seek government-supported security rather than to put faith in our own industry.[62]

JOHN A. WIDTSOE

The right of free agency is fundamental in the Gospel structure. Man should always be left free to accept or to reject. There should be no interference with the human will. If, under the eternal law, man chooses right, he is rewarded; if he chooses unwisely, he brings punishment upon himself. This doctrine was fought for and established in the Great Council held in the heavens before the earth was made.

This principle may be used in evaluating the merit of many social, economic, and political offerings of the day. Communism, Fascism, and Naziism may be judged by this principle—whatever endangers to the least degree man's right to act for himself is not of God and must be resisted by Latter-day Saints. The deep meaning of a constitutional form of government is that those who live under it shall determine its laws and policies, and then, knowing the consequences, be left free to obey or disobey the law.[63]

BRIGHAM YOUNG

My independence is sacred to me—it is a portion of that same Deity that rules in the heavens. There is not a being upon the face of the earth who is made in the image of God, who stands erect and is organized as God is, that should be deprived of the free exercise of his agency so far as he does not infringe upon others' rights, save by good advice and a good example.[64]

A man can dispose of his agency or of his birthright, as did Esau of old, but when disposed of he cannot again obtain it; consequently, it behooves us to be careful, and not forfeit the agency that is given to us. The difference between the righteous and the sinner, eternal life or death, happiness or misery, is this, to those who are exalted there are no bounds or limits to their privileges, their blessings have a continuation, and to their kingdoms, thrones, and dominions, principalities, and powers there is no end, but they increase through all eternity; whereas, those who reject the offer, who despise the proffered mercies of the Lord, and prepare themselves to be banished from His presence, and to become companions of the devils, have their agency abridged immediately, and bounds and limits are put to their operations.[65]

J. REUBEN CLARK JR.

So, brethren, I wish you to understand that *when we begin to tamper with the Constitution we begin to tamper with the law of Zion which God Himself set up*, and no one may trifle with the word of God with impunity.[66]

GEORGE ALBERT SMITH

I want to raise my voice to you and say, *our Heavenly Father raised up the very men that framed the Constitution of the United States*. He said He did. He gave to us the greatest Palladian of human rights that the world knows anything about, the only system whereby people could worship God according to the dictates of their consciences without, in any way, being molested when the law, itself, was in effect. . . . Yet, we have people who would like to change that and bring some of those forms of government that have failed absolutely to make peace and happiness and comfort any other place in the world, and exchange what God has given to us—the fullness of the earth and the riches of liberty and happiness. Yet, there are those who go around whispering and talking and saying, "Let us change this thing." I am saying to you that to me *the Constitution of*

CHAPTER FOUR

the United States of America is just as much from my Heavenly Father as the Ten Commandments. When that is my feeling, I am not going to go very far away from the Constitution, and I am going to *try to keep it where the Lord started it,* and not let anti-Christs come into this country that began because people wanted to serve God.[67]

In the next chapter, we will look at some areas of concern regarding the direction our government has taken the Constitution by promoting the idea that it is a living, breathing document subject to change. It is this, but only through the amendment process outlined in Article V, and not by congressional or judicial usurpations of power.

NOTES

1. Ernest L. Wilkinson, "The Changing Nature of American Government from a Constitutional Republic to a Welfare State" (Brigham Young University devotional, April 21, 1966).
2. *Teachings of the Prophet Joseph Smith,* arr. Joseph Fielding Smith (Salt Lake City: Deseret Book, 1938), 147.
3. John Taylor, in *Journal of Discourses,* 21:8.
4. Joseph Smith, in Ezra Taft Benson, "Our Divine Constitution," *Ensign,* November 1987.
5. Brigham Young, in *Journal of Discourses,* 7:14.
6. John Taylor, in Conference Report, April 8, 1883.
7. Wilford Woodruff, in Conference Report, April 1898.
8. *The Teachings of Lorenzo Snow,* comp. Clyde J. Williams (Salt Lake City: Bookcraft, 1984), 192.
9. Joseph F. Smith, in Conference Report, October 1912, 8.
10. Heber J. Grant, in Conference Report, October 1936, 6.
11. George Albert Smith, in Conference Report, April 1949.
12. David O. McKay, in Conference Report, October 1939.
13. Joseph Fielding Smith, in Conference Report, April 1943, 11–16.
14. Spencer W. Kimball, "Absolute Truth," *Ensign,* September 1978.
15. Ezra Taft Benson, in Conference Report, October 1944, 128–34.
16. Howard W. Hunter, "The Law of the Harvest: As a Man Sows, So Shall He Reap" (Brigham Young University devotional, March 8, 1966).

17. Gordon B. Hinckley, in "President Hinckley Addresses World Affairs Council," *Ensign*, August 1999.

18. Thomas S. Monson, at "Celebrate America," September 17, 2002.

19. Joseph Fielding Smith, in Conference Report, April 1950, 153–59.

20. *Journal of Discourses*, 6:152.

21. Joseph Fielding Smith, in Conference Report, April 1950, 159.

22. Joseph Smith, *General Smith's Views of the Powers and Policy of the Government of the United States* (Nauvoo, Illinois: John Taylor, 1844), http://www.latterdayconservative.com/joseph-smith/general-smiths -views-of-the-power-and-policy-of-the-government/.

23. Ibid.; emphasis added.

24. Ibid.; emphasis added.

25. Ibid.

26. Ibid.

27. John Taylor, in Conference Report, April 1882; John Taylor, in *Journal of Discourses*, 23:67.

28. Declaration of Independence; emphasis added.

29. Joseph Smith, *General Smith's Views of the Powers and Policy of the Government of the United States* (Nauvoo, Illinois: John Taylor, 1844), http://www.latterdayconservative.com/joseph-smith/general-smiths -views-of-the-power-and-policy-of-the-government/.

30. Ibid.

31. Ibid.

32. Brigham Young, in *Journal of Discourses*, 5:38, 232.

33. *Political Debates between Abraham Lincoln and Stephen A. Douglas* (Cleveland, Ohio: O. S. Hubbell and Company, 1895), 494.

34. Brigham Young, in *Journal of Discourses*, 5:38, 231–32.

35. Brigham Young, in *Journal of Discourses*, 12:204; emphasis added.

36. Brigham Young, in *Journal of Discourses*, 2:182.

37. Joseph Smith, in Ezra Taft Benson, "Our Divine Constitution," *Ensign*, November 1987.

38. Orson Hyde, in *Journal of Discourses*, 6:152; emphasis added.

39. Brigham Young, in *Journal of Discourses*, 7:15.

40. James Burgess, notebook, Church Archives; emphasis added. Joseph Smith, in "The Missouri Persecutions," *The Contributor*, 7:8, 284; emphasis added.

41. Joseph Smith, *Times and Seasons* 5:8 (April 15, 1844): 510.

42. "First Presidency Urges Observance of Bicentennial of the Constitution," 11.

43. Ezra Taft Benson, "The Constitution—A Heavenly Banner" (Brigham Young University speech, September 16, 1986), speeches.byu.edu.

44. Ezra Taft Benson, "Our Divine Constitution," *Ensign*, November 1987.

45. Ibid.

46. Ezra Taft Benson, "The Constitution—A Heavenly Banner" (Brigham Young University speech, September 16, 1986), speeches.byu.edu.

47. Ibid.

48. Ezra Taft Benson, "Our Divine Constitution," *Ensign*, November 1987.

49. David O. McKay, in Conference Report, October 1939.

50. James Burgess, notebook, Church Archives.

51. Orson Hyde, in *Journal of Discourses*, 6:152.

52. *Sermons and Missionary Services of Melvin J. Ballard*, comp. Bryant S. Hinckley (Salt Lake City: Deseret Book, 1949), 265.

53. Melvin J. Ballard, in Conference Report, 272.

54. Ezra Taft Benson, in Conference Report, October 1963, 16.

55. Albert E. Bowen, *The Church Welfare Plan* (Salt Lake City: The Church of Jesus Christ of Latter-day Saints, 1946), 14.

56. David O. McKay, "Widening and Extending Horizons," *Improvement Era*, February 1966, 92.

57. "David O. McKay: Ninth President of the Church," *President of the Church Student Manual* (2012), 146–63; emphasis in original.

58. David O. McKay, in Conference Report, April 1950, 32.

59. Henry D. Moyle, in Conference Report, October 1947, 46.

60. Ibid.

61. Marion G. Romney, in Conference Report, October 1968, 64–68.

62. Marion G. Romney, "The Perfect Law of Liberty," *Ensign*, November 1981.

63. John A. Widtsoe, "The Use of Gospel Standards," *Improvement Era*, August 1936, 489.

64. Brigham Young, in *Journal of Discourses*, 10:191.

65. Ibid.; 3:267.

66. J. Reuben Clark Jr., in Conference Report, October 1942, 58–59; emphasis added.

67. George Albert Smith, in Conference Report, April 1948, 182; emphasis added.

FIVE

More or Less than the Original Intent of the Constitution

Some 228 years after our constitutional, republican government was created, we need to realize that no free governmental system has lasted for more than about 200 years. The Founding Fathers recognized this fact from their study of history, and they knew that the government they created wouldn't last forever either. They had no illusions. They did their best, however, to fashion a government that would allow its citizens the greatest degree of liberty for the longest time possible. This they did by learning from the lessons of history.

JAMES MADISON

> They saw all the consequences in the principle, and they avoided the consequences by denying the principle.[1]

From these lessons of history, a new form of government was created, synthesized from all other forms of government, but unknown elsewhere at any time during the recorded history of the world. A constitutionally *limited* government consists of the following:

1. A vertical separation of powers (between the state and national governments):

CHAPTER FIVE

JAMES WILSON

A free government has often been compared to a pyramid. This allusion is made with peculiar propriety in the system before you; it is laid on the broad basis of the people; its powers gradually rise, while they are confined, in proportion as they ascend, until they end in that most permanent of all forms. When you examine all its parts, they will invariably be found to preserve that essential mark of free governments—a chain of connection with the people. Such, sir, is the nature of this system of government.[2]

THOMAS JEFFERSON

The way to have good and safe government is not to trust it all to one but to divide it among the many, distributing to everyone exactly the functions he is competent to. Let the national government be entrusted with the defense of the nation and its foreign and federal relations; the State governments with the civil rights, laws, police, and administration of what concerns the State generally; the counties with the local concerns of the counties, and each ward direct the interests within itself. It is by dividing and subdividing these republics from the great national one down through all its subordinations until it ends in the administration of every man's farm by himself, by placing under everyone what his own eye may superintend, that all will be done for the best.[3]

It is not by the consolidation, or concentration of powers, but by their distribution, that good government is effected. Were not this great country already divided into states, that division must be made, that each might do for itself what concerns itself directly, and what it can so much better do than a distant authority. Every state again is divided into counties, each to take care of what lies within its local bounds; each county again into townships or wards, to manage minuter details; and every ward into farms, to be governed each by its individual proprietor. . . . It is by this partition of cares, descending in gradation from general to particular, that the mass of human affairs may be best managed for the good and prosperity of all.[4]

2. A horizontal separation of powers (between the executive, legislative, and judicial branches of government):

> [Baron de] Montesquieu's basic contention was that those entrusted with power tend to abuse it; therefore, if governmental power is fragmented, each power will operate as a check on the others. In its usual operational form, one branch of government (the legislative) is entrusted with making laws, a second (the executive) with executing them, and a third (the judiciary) with resolving disputes in accordance with the law. . . . The framers [of our Constitution] carefully spelled out the independence of the three branches of government: executive, legislative, and judicial. At the same time, however, they provided for a system in which some powers should be shared: Congress may pass laws, but the president can veto them; the president nominates certain public officials, but Congress must approve the appointments; and laws passed by Congress as well as executive actions are subject to judicial review.[5]

3. The balancing effect of one type of government on another (e.g. democracy, republic, aristocracy, monarchy):

> The principle of separation of powers dates back as far as Aristotle's time. Aristotle favored a mixed government composed of monarchy, aristocracy, and democracy, seeing none as ideal, but a mix of the three useful by combining the best aspects of each.[6]

4. A government which is accountable to the people because of "voluntary" taxes:

ALEXANDER HAMILTON

> The amount to be contributed by each citizen will in a degree be at his own option, and can be regulated by an attention to his resources. . . . It is a signal advantage of taxes on articles of consumption, that they contain in their own nature a security against

> excess. . . . If duties are too high, they lessen the consumption; the collection is eluded; and the product to the treasury is not so great as when they are confined within proper and moderate bounds. This forms a complete barrier against any material oppression of the citizens by taxes of this class, and is itself a natural limitation of the power of imposing them. Impositions of this kind usually fall under the denomination of indirect taxes, and must for a long time constitute the chief part of the revenue raised in this country.[7]

5. One without a large standing army but with a state militia system requiring the states to support any war the national government enters:

JOHN ADAMS

> A Militia Law requiring all men, or with very few exceptions, besides cases of conscience, to be provided with arms and ammunition, to be trained at certain seasons, and requiring counties, towns, or other small districts to be provided with public stocks of ammunition and entrenching utensils, and with some settled plans for transporting provisions after the militia, when marched to defend their country against sudden invasions, and requiring certain districts to be provided with field-pieces, companies of matrosses and perhaps some regiments of light horse, is always a wise institution, and in the present circumstances of our country indispensible [sic].[8]

6. A government consisting of part-time, citizen-statesmen who live in their home districts and whose political responsibilities are secondary to their real-life pursuits:

> The Congress shall assemble at least once in every year, and such meeting shall be on the first Monday in December, unless they shall by law appoint a different day.[9]

> The Senators and Representatives shall receive a compensation for their services.[10]

The earliest members of Congress were compensated per diem.

7. A system based upon the Christian religion but without preference to any specific Christian church or denomination:

US SUPREME COURT

> There is no dissonance in these declarations. There is a universal language pervading them all, having one meaning. They affirm and reaffirm that this is a religious nation. These are not individual sayings, declarations of private persons. They are organic utterances. They speak the voice of the entire people. . . . This is a religious people. . . . This is a Christian nation.[11]

To come to this conclusion, the court examined thousands of documents concerning the founding of the nation, including state constitutions and compacts leading up to the Revolution.

BALANCING THE RIGHTS OF THE INDIVIDUAL WITH THE POWER OF THE MAJORITY

JAMES MADISON

> In the compound republic of America, the power surrendered by the people is first divided between two distinct governments, and then the portion allotted to each subdivided among distinct and separate departments. Hence a double security arises to the rights of the people. The different governments will control each other, at the same time that each will be controlled by itself. Second. It is of great importance in a republic not only to guard the society against the oppression of its rulers, but to guard one part of the society against the injustice of the other part. Different interests necessarily exist in different classes of citizens. If a majority be united by a common interest, the rights of the minority will be insecure.[12]

> To this manly spirit, posterity will be indebted for the possession, and the world for the example, of the numerous innovations displayed on the American theatre, in favor of private rights and

public happiness. Had no important step been taken by the leaders of the Revolution for which a precedent could not be discovered, no government established of which an exact model did not present itself, the people of the United States might, at this moment have been numbered among the melancholy victims of misguided councils, must at best have been laboring under the weight of some of those forms which have crushed the liberties of the rest of mankind. Happily for America, happily, we trust, for the whole human race, they pursued a new and more noble course. They accomplished a revolution which has no parallel in the annals of human society. They reared the fabrics of governments which have no model on the face of the globe. They formed the design of a great Confederacy, which it is incumbent on their successors to . . . perpetuate.[13]

ALEXANDER HAMILTON

The nature and extent of the powers as they are delineated in the Constitution. Every thing beyond this must be left to the prudence and firmness of the people; who, as they will hold the scales in their own hands, it is to be hoped, will always take care to preserve the constitutional equilibrium between the general [National] and the State governments. Upon this ground, which is evidently the true one, it will not be difficult to obviate the objections which have been made to an indefinite power of taxation in the United States.[14]

But as the plan of the convention aims only at a partial union or consolidation, the State governments would clearly retain all the rights of sovereignty which they before had, and which were not, by that act [the forming of the Constitution], *exclusively* delegated to the United States.[15]

What our Founding Fathers balanced in their creation was the *right* of the individual against the *power* of the majority. They feared the *majority* of a democracy as much as they feared a *king*.

JOHN ADAMS

> If a majority are capable of preferring their own private interest, or that of their families, counties, and *party*, to that of the nation collectively, some provision must be made in the constitution, in favor of justice, to compel all to respect the common right, the public good, the universal law, in preference to all private and partial considerations. . . . And that *the desires of the majority of the people are often for injustice and inhumanity against the minority*, is demonstrated by every page of the history of the whole world. . . . To remedy the dangers attendant upon the arbitrary use of power, checks, however multiplied, will scarcely avail without an *explicit admission of some limitation of the right of the majority to exercise sovereign authority over the individual citizen*. . . . In popular governments [democracies], minorities [individuals] constantly run much greater risk of suffering from arbitrary power than in absolute monarchies.[16]

> You have rights antecedent [existing before] to all earthly governments: rights that cannot be repealed or restrained by human laws; rights derived from the great Legislator of the universe.[17]

Our Founding Fathers started with the premise that we are all equal before God in the rights we possess, and therefore, should all be equal before the law. They realized that government was a creation of the people, and as such, held no moral right or power to do anything that any individual citizen could not morally do acting on their own. They set about to create a government whose purpose was to protect the individual rights of the creators. This they did through the creation of a social contract: the Constitution. They started by declaring their individual rights to life, liberty, and property in the Declaration of Independence. Then, in the Constitution, they outlined the limited powers to be given to government. The people then ratified the contract, and acknowledged their support for that government as long as it acted within the confines of the social contract. If government acted outside the bounds of that contract, it would lose the support of the people who were to sustain it, and the people could resort to their right to alter or abolish it.

THE OBLIGATION OF THE GOVERNMENT

Much has been said about the people's obligation to obey the law; enough has not been said, though, about the government's obligation to obey the law of the social contract it has with the people. The people are obliged to obey government at the threat of the loss of their property, their liberty, or their life. The government is obliged to honor the social contract by the threat of revolution, if it comes to that. The Founding Fathers warned their posterity of the dangers associated with *all* government and especially the danger of allowing a change in the government (the Constitution) by usurpation or the gradual encroachment of power by any level or branch of government. They knew that this would happen and therefore warned us about it.

Consider the following:

BENJAMIN FRANKLIN

[I] . . . believe farther that [this new government under the Constitution] can only end in Despotism, as other forms have done before it, when the people shall become so corrupted as to need despotic Government, being incapable of any other.[18]

In September of 1787, Benjamin Franklin, after emerging from Independence Hall following his signing of the Constitution, was asked by a lady, "Well Doctor what have we got a republic or a monarchy?" Franklin replied, "A republic . . . if you can keep it."[19]

JAMES MADISON

Since the general civilization of mankind, I believe there are more instances of the abridgment of the freedom of the people, by gradual and silent encroachments of those in power, than by violent and sudden usurpations.[20]

THOMAS JEFFERSON

> Whenever all government, domestic and foreign [referring to the roles of the state and national governments], in little as in great things, shall be drawn to Washington as the center of all power, it will render powerless the checks provided of one government on another and will become as venal and oppressive as the government from which we separated.[21]

JOHN DICKINSON

> Another truth respecting the vigilance with which a free people should guard their liberty, that deserves to be carefully observed, is this—that a *real tyranny* may prevail in a state, while the *forms* of a free constitution remain.[22]

ALEXANDER HAMILTON

> Government implies the power of making laws. It is essential to the idea of a law, that it be attended with a sanction; or, in other words, a penalty or punishment for disobedience. If there be no penalty annexed to disobedience, the resolutions or commands which pretend to be laws will, in fact, amount to nothing more than advice or recommendation. This penalty, whatever it may be, can only be inflicted in two ways: by the agency of the courts and ministers of justice, or by military force; by the *coercion* of the magistracy, or by the *coercion* of arms.[23]

The Founders knew what human nature would ultimately do to their creation. They knew that some elements of society would try to use this institution of force to subjugate other elements of society. There was never any doubt in their minds: they knew that their creation would ultimately be perverted, and eventually be destroyed like all other forms of government which preceded it

> When the people find that they can vote themselves money, that will herald the end of the republic.[24]

CHAPTER FIVE

> The democracy will cease to exist when you take away from those who are willing to work and give to those who would not.[25]

There seems to be two prevalent attitudes regarding government among the American people today. It is either (1) believed to be benevolent, and therefore, good; or (2) believed to be dangerous and destructive of the rights of the individual, and, therefore, must be carefully controlled and watched. One is historically correct, the other just wishful thinking. Government is no more benevolent than its imperfect human administrators.

JOHN ADAMS

> There is danger from all men. The only maxim of a free government ought to be to trust no man living with power to endanger the public liberty.[26]

ALEXANDER HAMILTON

> There is, in the nature of sovereign power, an impatience of control, that disposes those who are invested with the exercise of it, to look with an evil eye upon all external attempts to restrain or direct its operations. . . . This tendency is not difficult to be accounted for. It has its origin in the love of power. Power controlled or abridged is almost always the rival and enemy of that power by which it is controlled or abridged. This simple proposition will teach us how little reason there is to expect, that the persons entrusted with the administration of the affairs of the particular members of a confederacy will at all times be ready, with perfect good-humor, and an unbiased regard to the public weal, to execute the resolutions or decrees of the general authority. The reverse of this results from the constitution of human nature.[27]

JAMES MADISON

> Tyranny has perhaps oftener grown out of the assumptions of power, called for, on pressing exigencies, by a defective constitution, than out of the full exercise of the largest constitutional authorities.[28]

BENJAMIN FRANKLIN

> A nation of well informed men, who have been taught to know and prize the rights which God has given them, cannot be enslaved. It is in the region of ignorance alone that tyranny reigns.[29]

CONSTITUTIONAL CHANGES

After reading these quotes, it is worth taking a close look at our system of government to see if what the Founding Fathers thought was inevitable has, in fact, come to pass. What follows are fundamental changes that have been made to the system that the Founding Fathers created, and that our Heavenly Father endorsed in section 98 of the Doctrine and Covenants in 1833. We should ask ourselves the following questions as we consider the changes.

1.   Are all the checks and balances provided to us under the original intent of the social contract still in effect?
2.   Do we have the same level of individual liberty that our forefathers had?
3.   Was there something flawed that needed to be corrected in the document that Heavenly Father endorsed?
4.   Have we as Americans failed to maintain the principles provided to us by our Founding Fathers in the Constitution?

Keeping these questions in mind, we can see the following fundamental changes to the original Constitution:

1.   The Sixteenth Amendment's removal of the prohibition to access revenue through direct taxation, with the accompanying loss of governmental accountability.

2. The Seventeenth Amendment's removal of representation of state governments, as sovereign political entities, in the national government (the vertical separation of powers).

3. The lost right of the jury (the people) to decide matters of law and fact in criminal cases—thereby giving the people the final say on the enforcement of any law—by a Supreme Court ruling in 1895.

4. The lost right of the people to a sound financial system based on gold and silver, as specific by the Constitution, through the creation of the Federal Reserve System in 1913.

5. The lost right of the people to establish the "laws of the land" through a representative system, by the acceptance of executive orders, bureaucratic regulations, and judicial rulings as "law."

6. The lost rights of state and local governments given in the Ninth and Tenth Amendments to regulate their own affairs through the Federal Revenue Sharing Program, and the accompanying regulations regarding the use of monies.

7. The loss of a clear understanding of the Second Amendment: the rights of self-defense and the right to resist—the keystone of all individual rights guaranteed by the Constitution.

8. The application of the Federal Bill of Rights to the state governments through the interpretation contrary to original intent of the Thirteenth, Fourteenth, and Fifteenth Amendments by the Supreme Court.

9. The misapplication and interpretation of the "General Welfare" clause of the Constitution to mean that government has power to do virtually anything under the Constitution, instead of adhering to the original limitation of powers given therein.

10. The expansion of the national government, by the Supreme Court not honoring the written contract with the people for self-government, by interpreting laws based upon the "original intent" of the Constitution.

11. The establishment of (1) deficit spending, (2) the lack of a balanced federal budget, and (3) no governmental fiscal responsibility and accountability.

12. The establishment of an "imperial Congress," where Senators and members of Congress no longer live by the laws which they create, no longer live in the districts which they represent, and where they no longer work for their living.

13. The creation of "criminal" laws at the national level of government.

14. The loss of the understanding that this nation was founded upon the Christian religion.

A government fraught with fiscal irresponsibility, whose interest is in the pursuit of special-interest and power, that has no apparent respect for the rights of the individual citizen and the social contract that binds the people and their government together, cannot long survive if we are to accept the lessons of history. This is especially true when society no longer accepts absolute standards, such as the Ten Commandments and the teaching of Jesus Christ. We are currently seeing the political and moral destruction of the United States in the recent polls taken on the attitude of American citizens toward their government. According to some polls, "Only 29 percent trust the government to do what is right almost always or most of the time." And "nearly half . . . believe that the federal government threatens their personal rights and freedoms."[30] "The percentage of U.S. adults who see corruption as pervasive has never been less than a majority in the past decade."[31] "This year 53 percent of the poll's respondents answered 'yes' when asked if the federal government 'threatens your personal rights and freedoms.' This year's poll also found more people viewed the government as a 'major threat' than ever before."[32]

The next several chapters will go into more detail regarding major changes made to the Constitution given to us by our Founding Fathers, and which the Lord endorsed, comparing each change to the original intent using the words of the Founding Father's as our source for comparison.

CHAPTER FIVE

NOTES

1. James Madison, "Memorial and Remonstrance against Religious Assessments," address to Virginia General Assembly, June 20, 1785.
2. W. Cleon Skousen, *The Making of America: The Substance and Meaning of the Constitution* (Washington, D.C.: National Center for Constitutional Studies, 1985), 177.
3. Thomas Jefferson, quoted in Thomas Fleming, *The Politics of Human Nature* (London: Transaction Publishers, 1988), 202.
4. *Autobiography of Thomas Jefferson* (New York: G. P. Putnam's Sons, 1914), 122–23.
5. Xiaohong Wei, "How the US Constitution Separates National Power," *Varsity Tutors*, http://www.varsitytutors.com/earlyamerica/early-america-review/volume-13/constitution-separates-power.
6. Ibid.
7. Federalist Papers, no. 21.
8. John Adams, in *Classics of American Political and Constitutional Thought: Origins through the Civil War*, Scott J. Hammond, Kevin R. Hardwick, Howard L. Lubert, eds. (Indianapolis, Indiana: Hackett Publishing Company, 2007), 294.
9. US Constitution, Art. I, Sec. 4.
10. US Constitution, Art. I, Sec. 6.
11. US Supreme Court in Church of the Holy Trinity vs. United States, 1892, https://supreme.justia.com/cases/federal/us/143/457/case.html.
12. Federalist Papers, no. 51.
13. Federalist Papers, no. 14.
14. Federalist Papers, no. 31.
15. Federalist Papers, no. 32; emphasis added.
16. "On Government," in *The Works of John Adams*, vol. 5, comp. Charles Francis Adams (Boston, Massachusetts: Little, Brown, and Company, 1865), 8, 48, 490; emphasis added.
17. George Bancroft, "History of the United States from the Discovery of the American Continent," *Putnam's Monthly Magazine of American Literature, Science, and Art*, January to June, 1853, 307.
18. Max Farand, ed., *The Records of the Federal Convention of 1787*, vol. 2 (New Haven: Yale University Press, 1937), 642.
19. Max Farand, ed., *The Records of the Federal Convention of 1787*, vol. 3 (New Haven: Yale University Press, 1937), 85.

20. Suzy Platt, ed., *Respectfully Quoted: A Dictionary of Quotations* (Washington, D.C.: CQ Press, 1992), 523.

21. Thomas Jefferson to Charles Hammond, August 18, 1821, https://founders .archives.gov/documents/Jefferson/98-01-02-2260.

22. *The Political Writings of John Dickinson, Esquire*, vol. 2 (Wilmington: Bonsal and Niles, 1801), 291; emphasis in original.

23. Federalist Papers, no. 15; emphasis in original.

24. Attributed to Benjamin Franklin, but not verified; https://www.goodreads .com/quotes/88664-when-the-people-find-that-they-can-vote-themselves -money.

25. Attributed to Thomas Jefferson, but not verified; https://www.monticello .org/site/jefferson/democracy-will-cease-exist-quotation.

26. Notes for an Oration at Braintree (Spring, 1772), in *Diary and Autobiography of John Adams*, vol. 2 (1960).

27. Federalist Papers, no. 15.

28. Federalist Papers, no. 20.

29. Benjamin Franklin, *The Life of Benjamin Franklin, Written Chiefly by Himself*, rev. Mason L. Weems (Philadelphia: M. Carey, 1817), 84.

30. "Americans Distrust Government, but Want It to Do More," *NPR Online*, http://www.npr.org/programs/specials/poll/govt/summary.html.

31. "75% in U.S. See Widespread Government Corruption," *Gallup*, http:// www.gallup.com/poll/185759/widespread-government-corruption.aspx.

32. Seth Cline, "Poll: Most Americans Feel Threatened by Government," *U.S. News*, http://www.usnews.com/news/articles/2013/01/31/poll-most -americans-feel-threatened-by-government.

SIX

The National Government's Access to Revenue through Taxation

THOMAS PAINE

> The greedy hand of government thrusting itself into every corner and crevice of industry, and grasping the spoil of the multitude. Invention is continually exercised to furnish new pretenses for revenue and taxation. It watches prosperity as its prey, and permits none to escape without tribute.[1]

The Sixteenth Amendment, ratified in 1913, removed from the Constitution the strict limitation on the national government's ability to raise revenue, and hence, the influence that it could have in the lives of its citizens. In the original document, the national government could raise money by imposing indirect taxes only, such as duties, tariffs, imposts, and excise taxes. The only direct taxes it allowed were those that were apportioned equally among the states—meaning that the same amount would be raised from Delaware, one of the smallest states, as from Pennsylvania, one of the largest.

INDIRECT TAXATION

The Founders rejected the idea of direct taxation without apportionment in preference to indirect taxes which the people could *choose to pay* by what they chose to purchase. The American people, therefore, could control the amount of revenue that the government was raising through their choices in how they spent their dollars. It was recognized as a voluntary tax system. People only paid the tax if they chose to purchase the product which was taxed—much like our current "Gas Guzzler Tax" on cars with poor gas mileage. This gave each individual citizen the opportunity to "vote" each time they placed their hands into their pockets to make a purchase. This system provided a closed-loop feedback system whereby legislators knew fairly quickly what the people thought of the reasons for a tax, and/or the amount raised by the tax. How can we think we are voting today when we can only vote every two, four, or six years? The Constitution provided a system of true accountability for the national government to the states and to the people through the use of many different checks and balances. Funding through indirect taxes could only be raised when citizens chose to pay them by agreeing to purchase an item so taxed, and thereby agreeing to the purpose and the amount of the tax.

ALEXANDER HAMILTON

> Imposts, excises, and, in general, all duties upon articles of consumption . . . will, in time, find its level with the means of paying them. The amount to be contributed by each citizen will in a degree be at his own option, and can be regulated by an attention to his resources. The rich may be extravagant, the poor can be frugal; and private oppression may always be avoided by a judicious selection of objects proper for such impositions. . . . It is a signal advantage of taxes on articles of consumption, that they contain in their own nature a security against excess. They prescribe their own limit; which cannot be exceeded without defeating the end proposed, that is, an extension of the revenue. . . . If duties are too high, they lessen the consumption; the collection is eluded; and the product to the treasury is not so great as when they are confined within proper and moderate bounds. This forms a complete barrier against any material oppression of the citizens

by taxes of this class, and is itself a natural limitation of the power of imposing them. Impositions of this kind usually fall under the denomination of indirect taxes, and must for a long time constitute the chief part of the revenue raised in this country.[2]

The Founders realized the importance of individual choice as described by a twentieth-century legal theorist:

Business succeeds rather better than the state in imposing restraints upon individuals, because its imperatives are disguised as choices.[3]

Indirect taxation was *another level of checks and balances* provided by the Constitution: a check provided to the people directly on their government. This was actually a check upon a check because the members of the House of Representatives, who were democratically elected by the people, were the only ones in the government that could originate spending and taxation bills. With indirect taxation, the people, however, still had the final word on any tax law which Congress passed—because they could still exercise their right of choice in spending their dollars on goods which didn't have the tax on them. The Founding Fathers, with their concept of *limited* government, did not think that the national government needed access to *unlimited* funds. However, when it did, direct taxation, which was apportioned and difficult to get passed into law (because it required the same amount of money from each state without regard for population), could be used during times of emergency.

JAMES MADISON

Taxation will consist, in a great measure, of duties which will be involved in the regulation of commerce.[4]

A national revenue must be obtained; but the system must be such a one, that, while it secures the object of revenue, it shall not be oppressive to our constituents.[5]

THOMAS JEFFERSON

> To take from one, because it is thought that his own industry and that of his fathers has acquired too much, in order to spare to others, who, or whose fathers have not exercised equal industry and skill, is to violate arbitrarily the first principle of association.[6]

> At home, fellow citizens, you best know whether we have done well or ill. The suppression of unnecessary offices, of useless establishments and expenses, enabled us to discontinue our internal taxes. These covering our land with officers, and opening our doors to their intrusions, had already begun that process of domiciliary vexation which, once entered, is scarcely to be restrained from reaching successively every article of produce and property. . . . The remaining revenue on the consumption of foreign articles, is paid cheerfully by those who can afford to add foreign luxuries to domestic comforts, being collected on our seaboards and frontiers only, and incorporated with the transactions of our mercantile citizens, it may be the pleasure and pride of an American to ask, what farmer, what mechanic, what laborer, ever sees a tax-gatherer of the United States?[7]

ANDREW JACKSON

> Through the favor of an overruling and indulgent Providence our country is blessed with general prosperity and our citizens exempted from the pressure of taxation, which other less favored portions of the human family are obliged to bear.[8]

JAMES MADISON

> The apportionment of taxes on the various descriptions of property is an act which seems to require the most exact impartiality; yet there is, perhaps, no legislative act in which greater opportunity and temptation are given to a predominant party to trample on the rules of justice.[9]

CHAPTER SIX

ADAM SMITH

> Little else is requisite to carry a state to the highest degree of opulence from the lowest barbarism, but peace, *easy taxes*, and a tolerable administration of justice: all the rest being brought about by the natural course of things.[10]

THOMAS PAINE

> We still find the greedy hand of government thrusting itself into every corner and crevice of industry, and grasping the spoil of the multitude. Invention is continually exercised to furnish new pretenses for revenue and taxation. It watches prosperity as its prey, and permits none to escape without a tribute. . . .
>
> What at first was plunder, assumed the softer name of revenue.[11]

Our Founding Fathers included many different types of checks and balances into the Constitution—far more than the vertical and horizontal separation of powers that are the only ones taught today. Indirect taxes were an important check on government since it could not do much of anything without the ability to raise the funds.

DIRECT TAXATION

The ability of the federal government to *directly* tax the individual citizens of the United States *without* apportionment, by the Sixteenth Amendment, provided the government with unlimited access to the wealth of the nation. This was, obviously, not what the Founding Fathers intended. The idea of a direct-without-apportionment income tax on the individual citizen was not an unknown idea to them. They determined, though, that it would create a nation of "cheats and liars" and refused to utilize it. They also thought it necessary to provide the citizens with this immediate and important check on their government.

BARRY GOLDWATER

> The income tax created more criminals than any other single act of government.[12]

A new Gallup poll finds that a majority of Americans—52 percent—say they pay too much federal income tax.[13] And "just *45 percent of Americans have a favorable rating of the IRS*, compared with 48 percent who rate it unfavorably."[14]

Consider the following portion of the Constitution:

The Congress shall have power to lay and collect taxes, duties, imposts . . . ; but all duties, imposts and excises *shall be uniform* throughout the United States.[15]

How can this be reconciled with our current graduated income tax system? The Founders understood that government *had to be just* in order to be respected and, therefore, sustained by the people who actually held the right and power of self-government. A tax on individual citizens that is not uniform and not voluntary, is unfair and will ultimately undermine the people's faith in their government. This will ultimately lead to the revolution described in the Declaration of Independence: "When a long train of abuses and usurpations, pursuing invariably the same Object evinces [shows plainly] a design to reduce them under absolute Despotism."[16] Unchecked, government spending is quickly growing.

Though April 15 has passed, Americans are still a week away from the finish line when it comes to paying their taxes. This year, it will take the average American until April 24 to work enough to pay off their share of federal, state, and local taxes. We spend 30 percent of the year working to pay the government before we can start to keep the money that we earn.[17]

Another problem that we are facing with a graduated income tax was brought out in the following article from 1991:

The tax laws do not recognize inflation, and the inflation calculators do not recognize taxes. . . . Two illustrations make the point:
1. By official estimates, consumer inflation is at an annual rate under 5 percent. . . . But that . . . doesn't include taxes, which

have been rising at local, state and federal levels. Taxes, a major expense to most households, are simply excluded from consumer price index calculations.

2. Making matters worse, the income tax people decline to recognize the existence of inflation when levying your taxes. The Internal Revenue System does not care, for example, if the 6 percent you earn on a certificate of deposit is wiped out by 6 percent inflation. . . . Bad enough that taxes are rising; now you're taxed on income you never had.[18]

Now let's look at what the Founding Fathers had to say about taxation:

BENJAMIN FRANKLIN

They have power to make laws, and lay and levy such general duties, imports, or taxes, as to them shall appear most equal and just (considering the ability and other circumstances of the inhabitants in the several colonies), and such as may be collected with the least inconvenience to the people; rather discouraging luxury, than loading industry with unnecessary burdens.[19]

JAMES WILSON

In this Constitution, a power is given to Congress to collect imposts. . . . A very considerable part of the revenue of the United States will arise from that source; it is the easiest, most just, and most productive mode of raising revenue; and *it is a safe one, because it is voluntary.* No man is obliged to consume more than he pleases, and each buys in proportion only to his consumption.[20]

MR. NICHOLAS

Money cannot be raised in a more judicious manner than by imposts. . . . Were they raised by *direct taxes, they would be exceedingly oppressive.*[21]

ALEXANDER HAMILTON

> It is a signal advantage of taxes on articles of consumption [indirect taxes], that they contain in their own nature a security against excess. . . . If duties are too high, they lessen the consumption; the collection is eluded; and the product to the treasury is not so great as when they are confined within proper and moderate bounds. This forms a complete barrier against any material oppression of the citizen, by taxes of this class, and is itself a natural limitation of the power of imposing them.[22]

THOMAS JEFFERSON

> With money we will get men, said Caesar, and with men we will get money. Nor should our assembly [the Virginia Legislature] be deluded by the integrity of their own purposes, and conclude that these unlimited powers will never be abused, because themselves are not disposed to abuse them. They should look forward to a time, and that not a distant one, when a corruption in this, as in the country from which we derive our origin, will have seized the heads of government, and be spread by them through the body of the people; when they will purchase the voices of the people, and make them pay the price. Human nature is the same on every side of the Atlantic. . . . The time to guard against corruption and tyranny, is before they shall have gotten hold on us.[23]

Of the types of taxes available, the Founders chose the ones that would give the people the greatest degree of control over their government. They chose indirect taxes that are voluntary taxes paid by the people when they choose to purchase items that have a tax on them. Indirect taxes are also the best form of taxation if governmental accountability is desired because the people inform their representatives of what they think of the law every time they reach into their pockets to purchase something.

There are many types of taxes that the Founders considered, including direct taxes on a person's income, on his property, or on the individual himself, such as with a poll tax. The type of taxes they chose, however, were indirect taxes. These were *duties*—taxes on imports, exports, and/or manufactured goods; *tariffs*—taxes on imports and/or exports; *imposts*—taxes on imported articles at the moment of importation; and *excise taxes*—taxes on any article paid by the consumer or retailer at the time of purchase. These taxes were all voluntary: the citizen chose to pay them by choosing to purchase the items that had the tax placed on them. These were also very just taxes because the people with the most money, spent the most money, and hence, paid the most in taxes—voluntarily. This method of raising taxes was also very immediate. It didn't take Congress long to realize that the tax rate or tax purpose was not accepted by the people, because the people weren't making the purchases and paying the taxes. This was how the Founding Fathers provided the American citizens with a true feedback system to their government. No polling service was needed—and the results of a poll couldn't be manipulated by the way the questions were worded.

To add insult to injury, our present level of direct taxation we now labor under is estimated to be ten thousand times the level of taxation that the Founders fought the revolution over!

NOTES

1. Thomas Paine, *Rights of Man* (1791).
2. Federalist Papers, no. 21.
3. Walton Hale Hamilton, in Robert W. McChesney, *Telecommunications, Mass Media, and Democracy* (New York: Oxford University Press, 1993), 97.
4. Federalist Papers, no. 56.
5. James G. Blaine, "Twenty Years of Congress," vol. 1 (1884), 185; William H. Michael and Pitman Pulsifer, comps., *Tarif Acts Passed by the Congress of the United States from 1789 to 1895* (Washington: Government Printing Office, 1896), 2.
6. Andrew A. Lipscomb and Albert Ellery Bergh, eds., *The Writings of Thomas Jefferson* (Washington: Thomas Jefferson Memorial Association, 1905).
7. Thomas Jefferson, second inaugural address, March 4, 1805.

8. Andrew Jackson, veto message regarding funding of infrastructure development, May 27, 1830.

9. Federalist Papers, no. 10.

10. Dugald Stewart, *Account of the Life and Writings of Adam Smith* (1793), 25.

11. Thomas Paine, *Rights of Man* (1791).

12. Benny L. Kass, "Too-Good-to-Be-True Tax Myths," *Washington Post*, January 5, 2008.

13. Susan Jones, "Gallup: 52% of Americans Say Federal Income Taxes Too High," *CNSNews.com*, April 15, 2014, http://cnsnews.com/news/article /susan-jones/gallup-52-americans-say-federal-income-taxes-too-high.

14. Seth Motel, "5 Facts on How Americans View Taxes," *Pew Research Center*, April 10, 2015, http://www.pewresearch.org/fact-tank /2015/04/10/5-facts-on-how-americans-view-taxes/.

15. US Constitution, Art. I, Sec. 8; emphasis added.

16. Declaration of Independence.

17. Jared Meyer, "Working for the Tax Man," *U.S. News*, April 16, 2015, http://www.usnews.com/opinion/economic-intelligence/2015/04/16/tax -day-doesnt-mean-americans-are-done-working-to-pay-off-tax-burden.

18. John Cunniff, "Inflation, Taxes Deal a Double Whammy," *Deseret News*, June 3, 1991, http://www.deseretnews.com/article/165597/INFLATION -TAXES-DEAL-A-DOUBLE-WHAMMY.html?pg=all.

19. Benjamin Franklin, "The Albany Plan of Union, July 1754," in *The Papers of Benjamin Franklin*, ed. Leonard W. Labaree (New Haven: Yale University Press, 1959).

20. James Wilson, in Jonathan Elliot, *The Debates in the Several State Conventions on the Adoption of the Federal Constitution as Recommended by the General Convention at Philadelphia in 1787*, vol. 2 (New York: Burt Franklin), 467; emphasis added.

21. Mr. Nicholas, in Jonathan Elliot, *The Debates in the Several State Conventions on the Adoption of the Federal Constitution as Recommended by the General Convention at Philadelphia in 1787*, vol. 3 (New York: Burt Franklin), 99; emphasis added.

22. Federalist Papers, no. 21.

23. Thomas Jefferson, *Notes on the State of Virginia*, ed. William Peden (Chapel Hill: University of North Carolina Press, 1954).

SEVEN

State Governments vs. the National Government

JAMES MADISON

> There is a peculiarity in the federal Constitution which insures a watchful attention in a majority both of the people and of their representatives to a constitutional augmentation of the latter. The peculiarity lies in this, that one branch of the legislature is a representation of citizens, the other of the States.[1]

We inaccurately think that the people created a *democracy* when the Constitution was created. The Constitution was actually created by the states and then ratified by the people through the Constitutional Conventions, which prevented members of the states who created the document from ratifying it. Today, we think of the United States of America as being one entity; the Founders thought of it as the several states forming one national government. This is a subtle difference, but it's very instructive: the states were sovereign within their spheres and created the national government to only do what they could not do for themselves. The way the states protected themselves from an over-reaching national government was to have the state governments represented as sovereign political entities in the Senate of the national government, and requiring that all bills had to be accepted by the Senate before being sent to the president for signature or veto.

CREATING A NEW SYSTEM OF GOVERNMENT

The Founding Fathers surveyed the various forms of government that were found throughout the world, as well as, those that could be found during the ancient Israelite, Greek, and Roman periods of history. They found that there were four predominant forms of government: (1) a democracy, (2) a republic, (3) an aristocracy, and (4) a monarchy. They also found that each of these forms of government had their positive and negative elements. A *democracy* was positive in that it provided the people who created the government with a voice in its affairs: in a democracy, the power to govern was justly derived from the consent of the people. It was, however, unworkable with a large geographically diverse population, and there was no guarantee of individual rights—since the majority ruled. A *republic* provided the people with a voice in choosing their representatives and was workable for large populations but it was prone to corruption because the government was too far removed from the people. Typically there was no guarantee of individual rights (personal and property) in a republic, since the representatives had to reflect the will of the majority in order to obtain reelection. An *aristocracy* was effective in protecting property rights because most of the property was owned by the aristocracy that ruled. It was also good in the fact that those who governed were more experienced in business and with human nature. The negative points of an aristocracy were that all the people didn't have voting rights, and there was no guarantee of individual rights for the common man. A *monarchy* proved to be quite an effective form of government during times of war or crisis since there were no long debates trying to arrive at a consensus. However, there were no guarantees to property or individual rights, the people were not given the opportunity to vote and be represented, and were usually barred from even voicing their opinions.

From these four different political systems, the Founders synthesized a new political system that included all the positive elements, and avoided the negative elements, of each form of government. This is one of the things that made our government so unique. When a negative element of government could not be altogether avoided, checks and balances were placed in the new political system to limit them. These checks and balances included: (1) three branches of government to check each other (legislative, executive, and judicial), (2) two levels of government with defined powers checking each other (state and national), (3) juries made up of the people having the final say on the application of the law, (4) indirect taxes so the people could constantly be "voting" with their dollars, and (5) the check and balance of each of the forms of government on the other forms of government, making up the whole.

A written constitution was important to the Founders because it provided a written representation of the social contract that the people "signed," which empowered the government. It also provided written guarantees regarding how the individual citizens were to be treated by that government, if there was conflict between them. The four forms of government mentioned previously were incorporated into our American constitutional system. The executive branch with its emergency powers represents the monarchical form of government. The House of Representatives containing the only representatives that the people elect directly represents the democratic form of government. The Senate, with members being chosen by the state legislatures, and not the people, represented the aristocratic form of government. The entire government was established using the republican model. It is interesting to note that the Constitution empowered only the House of Representatives to initiate spending bills—the democratic arm of government representing the people would have to pay the bills. Also of interest, is the fact that the Senate had to pass any bill coming out of the democratic chamber to ensure that the rights of the states were not being usurped by the national government. Also, the Senate was given the responsibility to oversee (ratify) treaties made by the executive branch, and to ratify Supreme Court justices proposed by the president. Senators were usually older, more experienced individuals who were chosen by their state legislatures because of their wisdom, knowledge, and experience (this is no longer true, however).

Originally, Senators were not elected democratically by the citizens of the state that they represented (like Congressmen), but were elected by the state legislatures and sent to Washington, D.C. to represent the state as a political entity of its own. The Senators' primary function was to preserve the delicate balance created by the Constitution, in the vertical separation of powers between the state and the national governments. As late as the 1930s, it was understood and accepted that only the state governments had the right and power to legislate in the areas of "domestic" concern, such as, education, welfare, safety, business regulation, banking, insurance, health, and so on. The powers of the national government were restricted by the Constitution itself, and the Tenth Amendment, to those areas of concern that the states *could not deal with for themselves*; such as, waging war, negotiating peace and commerce treaties, providing a postal service and National Bureau of Standards, and controlling commerce between the states (so that states couldn't place tariffs on the products of sister states). The national government also regulated the interstate and international waterways.

The Founding Fathers found it necessary to have not only the people, but also the territory represented. That is why the members of the House of Representatives were elected by the people, and the Senators were elected by the state legislatures and sent to the federal level of government to represent the states as territories and independent political entities.

JAMES MADISON

> But it is not possible to give to each department an equal power of self-defense. In republican government, the legislative authority necessarily predominates. The remedy for this inconveniency is to divide the legislature into different branches; and to render them, by different modes of election and different principles of action, as little connected with each other as the nature of their common functions and their common dependence on the society

will admit. It may even be necessary to guard against dangerous encroachments by still further precautions. . . .

In the compound republic of America, the power surrendered by the people is *first* divide between two distinct governments, and then the portion allotted to each subdivided among distinct and separate departments. Hence a double security arises to the rights of the people. The different governments will control each other, at the same time that each will be controlled by itself. . . .

It is of great importance in a republic not only to guard the society against the oppression of its rulers, but to guard one part of the society against the injustice of the other part. . . . Whilst all authority in [the federal republic] will be derived from and dependent on the society, the society itself will be broken into so many parts, interests, and classes of citizens, that the rights of individuals, or of the minority, will be in little danger from interested combinations of the majority.[2]

The Senate, on the other hand, will derive its powers from the States, as political and coequal societies; and these will be represented on the principle of equality in the Senate.[3]

The powers delegated by the proposed Constitution to the federal government are *few* and defined.[4]

The Accumulation of all powers, legislative, executive, and judiciary, in the same hands, whether of one, a few, or many, and whether hereditary, self-appointed, or *elective*, may justly be pronounced the very definition of tyranny.[5]

The House of Representatives . . . can make no law which will not have its full operation on *themselves* and their friends, as well as on the great mass of the society.[6]

The propriety of these distinctions is explained by the nature of the senatorial trust, which, requiring greater extent of information and stability of character, requires at the same time that the senator should have reached a period of life most likely to supply these advantages; and which, participating immediately in transactions with foreign nations, ought to be exercised by none who are not thoroughly weaned from the prepossessions and habits incident to foreign birth and education. . . . It is equally unnecessary to dilate on the appointment of senators by the State legislatures. Among the various modes which might have been devised for constituting this branch of the government, that which has been proposed by the convention is probably the most congenial with the public opinion. It is recommended by the double advantage of favoring a select appointment, and of giving to the State governments such an agency in the formation of the federal government as must secure the authority of the former, and may form a convenient link between the two systems.[7]

First. It is a misfortune incident to republican government, though in a less degree than to other governments, that those who administer it may forget their obligations to their constituents, and prove unfaithful to their important trust. In this point of view, a senate, as a second branch of the legislative assembly, distinct from, and dividing the power with, a first, must be in all cases a salutary check on the government. It doubles the security to the people, by requiring the concurrence of two distinct bodies in schemes of usurpation or perfidy, where the ambition or corruption of one would otherwise be sufficient. . . . Secondly. The necessity of a senate is not less indicated by the propensity of all single and numerous assemblies to yield to the impulse of sudden and violent passions, and to be seduced by factious leaders into intemperate and pernicious resolutions. Examples on this subject might be cited without number.[8]

Allow me, my dear sir, to express on this occasion, what I always feel, an anxious hope that, as our Constitution rests on a middle ground between a form wholly national and one merely federal, and on a division of the powers of Government between the States in their united character and in their individual characters, this peculiarity of the system will be kept in view, as a key to the sound interpretation of the instrument, and a warning against any doctrine that would either enable the States to invalidate the [constitutional] powers of the United States, or confer all power on them.[9]

ALEXANDER HAMILTON

That through the medium of the State legislatures which are select bodies of men, and which are to appoint the members of the national Senate there is reason to expect that this branch will generally be composed with peculiar care and judgment; that these circumstances promise greater knowledge and more extensive information in the national councils, and that they will be less apt to be tainted by the spirit of faction, and more out of the reach of those occasional ill-humors, or temporary prejudices and propensities, which, in smaller societies, frequently contaminate the public councils, beget injustice and oppression of a part of the community, and engender schemes which, though they gratify a momentary inclination or desire, terminate in general distress, dissatisfaction, and disgust.[10]

It is certainly true that the State legislatures, by forbearing the appointment of senators, may destroy the national government. But it will not follow that, because they have a power to do this in one instance, they ought to have it in every other. There are cases in which the pernicious tendency of such a power may be far more decisive, without any motive equally cogent with that which must have regulated the conduct of the convention in respect to the formation of the Senate, to recommend their admission into the system. So far as that construction may expose the Union to the possibility of injury from the State legislatures, it is an evil; but it is an evil which could not have been avoided without excluding the States, in their political capacities, wholly from a place in the organization of the national government. If this had been done, it would doubtless have been interpreted into an entire dereliction of the federal principle; and would certainly have deprived the State governments of that absolute safeguard which they will enjoy under this provision.[11]

The dissimilar modes of constituting the several component parts of the government. The House of Representatives being to be elected immediately by the people, the Senate by the State legislatures.[12]

This balance between the national and State governments ought to be dwelt on with peculiar attention, as it is of the *utmost importance*. It forms a double security to the people. If one encroaches on their rights, they will find a powerful protection in the other. Indeed, they will both be prevented from overpassing their constitutional limits, by certain rivalship, which will ever subsist between them.[13]

JOHN ADAMS

If a majority are capable of preferring their own private interest, or that of their families, counties, and party, to that of the nation collectively, some provision must be made in the constitution, in favor of justice, to compel all to respect the common right, the public good, the universal law, in preference to all private and partial considerations. . . . And that the desires of the majority of the people are often for injustice and inhumanity against the minority, is demonstrated by every page of history. . . . To remedy the dangers attendant upon the arbitrary use of power, checks, however multiplied, will scarcely avail without an explicit admission of some limitation of the right of the majority to exercise sovereign authority over the individual citizen. . . . In popular governments, minorities constantly run much greater risk of suffering from arbitrary power than in absolute monarchies.[14]

Democracy . . . while it lasts is more bloody than either aristocracy or monarchy. Remember, democracy never lasts long. It soon wastes, exhausts, and murders itself. There is never a democracy that did not commit suicide.[15]

THOMAS JEFFERSON

The true barriers [supports] of our liberty in this country are our State governments; and the wisest conservative power ever contrived by man is that of which our Revolution and present government found us possessed.[16]

The state governments . . . [are] the most competent administrations for our domestic concerns and the surest bulwarks against anti-republican tendencies.[17]

We can see, from the previous quotations, that our Founding Fathers created a confederated, or federal, government where the powers given to the various governments—national, state, county, and town—were appropriate for that level of government, and where the services provided were provided by that government closest to the people, and therefore, the most accountable to the people. The Seventeenth Amendment removed from our federal government a critical check and balance that allowed for the maintenance of this principle. Since the ratification of the Seventeenth Amendment, we have seen an uncontrolled growth of the national government.

Since there is no longer a chamber of the national government to prevent their usurpation of powers from the state governments, in 2016 we had 438 agencies listed in the National Register of the United States Government, which writes regulations to control all aspects of American life. CNS News now tells us, "The BLS [Bureau of Labor Statistics] has published seasonally-adjusted month-by-month employment numbers for both government and manufacturing going back to 1939. In the first 50 years of the 76-year span since then, manufacturing out-employed government. But in August 1989, government overtook manufacturing as a U.S. employer. That month, government employed 17,989,000 and manufacturing employed 17,964,000. Since then, government employment has increased 4,006,000 and manufacturing employment has declined 5,635,000. . . . The 21,995,000 employed by government in August 2015 equaled 1 for each 14.6 people in the overall population of 321,191,461."[18]

And what is it that all these good people in government are doing for the United States economy and their citizens? According to the Competitive Enterprise Institute,

> Federal regulation and intervention cost American consumers and businesses an estimated $1.88 trillion in 2014 in lost economic productivity and higher prices. If U.S. federal regulation was a country, it would be the world's tenth largest economy. . . . Economy-wide regulatory costs amount to an average of $14,976 per household—around 29 percent of an average family budget of $51,100. Although not paid directly by individuals, this "cost" of regulation exceeds the amount an average family spends on health care, food and transportation. The "Unconstitutionality Index" is the ratio of regulations issued by unelected agency officials compared to legislation enacted by Congress in a given year. In 2014, agencies issued 16 new regulations for every law—that's 3,554 new regulations compared to 224 new laws. Many Americans complain about taxes, but regulatory compliance costs exceed what the IRS is expected to collect in both individual and corporate income taxes for last year—by more than $160 billion.[19]

The author from the previous article, Clyde Wayne Crews, and Ryan Young from the *American Spectator*, coauthored the following article that I have quoted from. They agreed that "Twenty years ago saw the release of the first edition of *Ten Thousand Commandments*, an annual report that tracks the cost and scope of the federal regulatory state." They continue, "It's been a very busy two decades for Washington, with 81,883 new regulations hitting the books during that time. That's a new regulation every two hours and nine minutes—24 hours per day, 365 days per year, for 20 years. . . . As the just-released 20th anniversary edition of *Ten Thousand Commandments* shows, every year, agencies continue to issue thousands of regulations costing billions of dollars. . . . The total estimated burden is now up to $1.8 trillion *per year*. . . . The number of specific regulatory restrictions listed in the *Code of Federal Regulations* (CFR) topped one million in 2010. . . . The most recent print edition contains 174,545 thrilling pages. . . . The number of individual regulatory restrictions in the CFR topped one million in 2010." Crews and Young go on to suggest that we implement a Regulatory Reduction Commission or that we require "every new regulation to automatically sunset after five years. Just as milk cartons have expiration dates, so should regulations."[20]

According to Penny Starr of CNS News, during the Obama administration alone, 11,327 pages of federal regulations were added, as of September 10, 2012.[21]

JAMES MADISON

> First. It is a misfortune incident to republican government, though in a less degree than to other governments, that those who administer it may forget their obligations to their constituents, and prove unfaithful to their important trust. In this point of view, a Senate, as a second branch of the legislative assembly, distinct from, and dividing the power with, a first, must be in all cases a salutary check on the government. It doubles the security to the people, by requiring the concurrence of two distinct bodies in schemes of usurpation or perfidy, where the ambition or corruption of one would otherwise be sufficient. This is a precaution founded on such clear principles, and now so well understood in the United States, that it would be more than superfluous to enlarge on it. I will barely remark, that as the improbability of sinister combinations will be in proportion to the dissimilarity in the genius of the two bodies, it must be politic to distinguish them from each other by every circumstance.[22]

> Many of these federal agencies are not accountable to the President, the Congress, or to the people of the United States. These agencies have quasi-legislative and judicial powers once they have

been created; setting their own regulations and settling their own disputes with the public. They are, in effect, a fourth branch of government, without checks and balances, without a separation of powers, without conformity to the principles of our Founding Fathers, and unaccountable to the people they are supposed to serve.[23]

NOTES

1. Federalist Papers, no. 58.
2. Federalist Papers, no. 51; emphasis added.
3. Federalist Papers, no. 39.
4. Federalist Papers, no. 45; emphasis added.
5. Federalist Papers, no. 47; emphasis added.
6. Federalist Papers, no. 57; emphasis added.
7. Federalist Papers, no. 62.
8. Ibid.
9. Letter from James Madison to Andrew Stevenson, November 27, 1830, in *Letters and Other Writings of James Madison* (J. B. Lippincott and Co., 1865).
10. Federalist Papers, no. 27.
11. Federalist Papers, no. 59.
12. Federalist Papers, no. 60.
13. Alexander Hamilton, in *American Eloquence: A Collection of Speeches and Addresses by the Most Eminent Orators of America*, vol. 1, ed. Frank Moore (New York: D. Appleton and Company, 1880), 194.
14. "On Government," in *The Works of John Adams*, vol. 5, comp. Charles Francis Adams (Boston, Massachusetts: Little, Brown, and Company, 1865), 8, 48, 490.
15. Letter from John Adams to John Taylor, 1814.
16. Letter from Thomas Jefferson to Destutt de Tracy, 1811.
17. Thomas Jefferson, second inaugural address, March 4, 1801.
18. Terence P. Jeffrey, "21,995,000 to 12,329,000: Government Employees Outnumber Manufacturing Employees 1.8 to 1," *CNSNews.com*, September 8, 2015, http://cnsnews.com/news/article/terence-p-jeffrey/21955000-1232 9000-government-employees-outnumber-manufacturing.

19. Clyde Wayne Crews, "Ten Thousand Commandments 2015," *Competitive Enterprise Institute*, May 8, 2015, https://cei.org/10kc2015?utm_source =google&utm_medium=cpc&utm_campaign=GoogleGrants&gclid =Cj0KEQjwiKS3BRCU-7XQ75Te3NoBEiQAA2t_xKUfcwKtH 05dg5NG3U5EGUuLfAIddwRDbKdILxFa9F4aAl_M8P8HAQ.

20. Clyde Wayne Crews and Ryan Young, "Twenty Years of Non-Stop Regulation," *The American Spectator*, June 5, 2013, http://spectator.org /articles/55475/twenty-years-non-stop-regulation.

21. Penny Starr, "Under Obama, 11,327 Pages of Federal Regulations Added," *CNSNews.com*, September 10, 2012, http://cnsnews.com/news/article /under-obama-11327-pages-federal-regulations-added.

22. Federalist Papers, no. 62.

23. W. David Stedman and Lavaughn G. Lewis, eds., *Our Ageless Constitution* (National Book Network, 1987), 100–101.

EIGHT

The Lost Right of the Jury

WILLIAM PULTENEY

> For twelve honest men have decided the cause, Who are judges alike of the facts and the laws.[1]

THOMAS JEFFERSON

> The opinion which gives to the judges the right to decide what laws are constitutional and what not, not only for themselves in their own sphere of action but for the Legislature and Executive also in their spheres, would make the Judiciary a despotic branch.[2]

> It is not only vain, but wicked, in a legislator to frame laws in opposition to the laws of nature, and to arm them with the terrors of death. This is truly creating crimes in order to punish them.[3]

Originally, under the Constitution, and prior to that in the colonies and going back through centuries of English Common Law history, the jury had the right and power to decide matters of law as they related to a case, as well as, the matters of fact involved in the specific case. This is what was meant by "trial by jury" as one Supreme Court Justice pointed out in the dissenting opinion of the court during Sparf and Hansen vs. United States.[4] Only a jury of your peers with this full

106

right intact, could remove from a citizen their life, liberty, or property. The jury had the right and obligation to determine the facts of the case—did the accused commit the crime he or she was charged with—but also the right and power to say the law was unjust and they were not going to punish a fellow citizen because of it. This full right of the jury also prevented "esprit de corps"—being puffed up with their own importance—amongst judges because it was clearly understood that they were to serve as a counselor to the jury regarding points of law. The judge, however, was not to be the final word: the jury could choose to disregard the judge's recommendation. This also prevented judges from becoming too inflexible, harsh in their rulings, or overly strict in their interpretation of the law; because the jury ultimately decided, not the judge. The jury had the right and power to disregard the law as explained by the judge and make their own ruling as their sworn duty to the Constitution and their consciences required.

The beauty of this system was that it provided a full circle of accountability: from the sovereign people to the legislators who created the laws on the people's behalf, to the executive department who enforced the law as written by the legislature, to the judicial system who tried citizens for alleged infringements of the law, and ultimately back to the people in the form of the jury—fellow citizens who had been called to judge another citizen based on the evidence provided, and called to judge the law based on their conscience. Through the jury, the people—who created, empowered, financed, and sustained government—had the final say on the laws that were enacted and how they were interpreted and enforced on a case-by-case basis.

Through this system, there was also no danger of the establishment of "judicial precedence." Each case was tried on *its* merits and not affected by the mistakes or prejudices of earlier judicial rulings: each jury was brand new, each case unique, each individual equal before the law. All of this changed with a 1895 Supreme Court ruling that removed from the jury the right to decide the law as it pertained to each case. The jury became the servant of the judge, instead of the servant of the people. Here is part of the dissenting opinion of the court on this issue:

> It is our deep and settled conviction, . . . that the jury, upon the general issue of guilty or not guilty in a criminal case, have the right, as well as the power, to decide, according to their own judgment and consciences, all questions, whether of law or of fact, involved in that issue. . . . If the judge's opinion in matter of law must rule the issue of fact submitted to the jury, the trial by jury would be useless.[5]

Lord Chatham said to the House of Lords regarding trial by jury under British Common Law (the source of US Common Law): "This, my lords, I never understood to be the law of England, but the contrary. I always understood that the jury were competent judges of the law as well as the fact; and indeed, if they were not, I can see no essential benefit from their institution to the community."[6]

ALEXANDER HAMILTON

> The friends and adversaries of the plan of the convention, if they agree in nothing else, concur at least in the value they set upon the trial by jury; or if there is any difference between them it consists in this: the former regard it as a valuable safeguard to liberty; the latter represent it as the very palladium of free government. For my own part, the more the operation of the institution has fallen under my observation, the more reason I have discovered for holding it in high estimation.[7]

> That in the general distribution of powers in our system of jurisprudence. . . . That in criminal cases, the law and fact being always blended, *the jury*, for reasons of a political and peculiar nature, *for the security of life and liberty*, is entrusted with the power of deciding *both law and fact*.[8]

CHAPTER EIGHT

THEOPHILUS PARSONS

The people themselves have it in their power effectually to resist usurpation, without being driven to an appeal to arms. An act of usurpation is not obligatory; it is not law; and any man may be justified in his resistance. Let him be considered as a criminal by the general government, yet only his own fellow-citizens can convict him; they are his jury, and if they pronounce him innocent, not all the powers of Congress can hurt him; and innocent they certainly will pronounce him, if the supposed law he resisted was an act of usurpation.[9]

PATRICK HENRY

Why do we love this trial by jury? Because it prevents the hand of oppression from cutting you off. . . . Has not your mother country magnanimously preserved this noble privilege upwards of a thousand years? . . . This gives me comfort—that, as long as I have existence, my neighbors will protect me.[10]

ALEXANDER HAMILTON

This is jurisdiction of both fact and law; nor is it even possible to separate them. Though the common-law courts of this State ascertain disputed facts by a jury, yet they unquestionably have jurisdiction of both fact and law; and accordingly when the former is agreed in the pleadings, they have no recourse to a jury, but proceed at once to judgment.[11]

This is not the situation in which we find ourselves today: the jury no longer has the right to decide matters of law. I have been on two juries in two different states, and in each case the last question asked of the jury members, before being seated by the judge, was a question to the effect, "Do you have a problem with confining your decisions to matters of fact, and allowing me [the judge] to determine all matters of the law?" I never raised my hand to say that I had a problem with it, knowing what the outcome would be for me, but surely this is not how the Founding Fathers envisioned the jury system.

NOTES

1. William Pulteney, quoted in John Townshend, *A Treatise on the Wrongs Called Slander and Libel, and on the Remedy by Civil Action for Those Wrongs* (New York: Baker, Voorhis, and Co., Law Publishers, 1877), 119.
2. Letter from Thomas Jefferson to Abigail Adams, 1804.
3. John P. Foley, ed., *The Jeffersonian Cyclopedia: A Comprehensive Collection of the Views of Thomas Jefferson* (New York: Funk and Wagnalls Company, 1900), 486.
4. Sparf and Hansen vs. United States, 1895, https://supreme.justia.com/cases/federal/us/156/51/case.html.
5. Ibid.
6. Lord Chatham, December 5, 1770, quoted in Sparf and Hansen vs. United States, 1895, https://supreme.justia.com/cases/federal/us/156/51/case.html.
7. Federalist Papers, no. 83.
8. Sparf and Hansen vs. United States, 1895, https://supreme.justia.com/cases/federal/us/156/51/case.html; emphasis added.
9. Theophilus Parsons in Jonathan Elliot, *The Debates in the Several State Conventions on the Adoption of the Federal Constitution as Recommended by the General Convention at Philadelphia in 1787*, vol. 2 (New York: Burt Franklin), 93–94.
10. Patrick Henry in Jonathan Elliot, *The Debates in the Several State Conventions on the Adoption of the Federal Constitution as Recommended by the General Convention at Philadelphia in 1787*, vol. 4 (New York: Burt Franklin), 144–45.
11. Federalist Papers, no. 81.

NINE

The Lost Right to Sound Monetary Policy

I t is well enough that people of the nation do not understand our banking and monetary system, for if they did, I believe there would be a revolution before tomorrow morning."[1]

"Let us control the money of a country and we care not who makes its laws." This is the maxim of the house of Rothschilds, and is the foundation of European banks.[2]

ALAN GREENSPAN, FORMER CHAIR OF FEDERAL RESERVE

In the absence of the gold standard, there is no way to protect savings from confiscation through inflation. There is no safe store of value. If there were, the government would have to make its holding illegal, as was done in the case of gold. If everyone decided, for example, to convert all his bank deposits to silver or copper or any other good, and thereafter decline to accept checks as payment for goods, bank deposits would lose their purchasing power and government-created bank credit would be worthless as a claim on goods. The financial policy of the welfare state requires that there be no way for the owners of wealth to protect themselves. This is the shabby secret of the welfare statists' tirades against gold. . . . Deficit spending is simply a scheme for the confiscation of wealth.

Gold stands in the way of this insidious process. It stands as a pro-
tector of property rights. If one grasps this, one has no difficulty in
understanding the statists' antagonism toward the gold standard.[3]

The Constitution gives Congress the power "to coin money, regulate the value thereof, and of foreign coin.[4] . . . No state shall . . . coin
money; emit bills of credit; make any thing but *gold and silver* coin a
tender in payment of debts."[5]

It is clear that the Founding Fathers intended us to have specie or
commodity money—coins which had intrinsic value in the metal they
contained.

THE TYPES AND VALUES OF MONEY

There are three types of money: commodity, representative, and fiat
money. Commodity money, such as a coin, also known as specie, has
intrinsic value because of the value of the metal used to coin the money;
representative money is a note which represents the commodity money
and can be redeemed for such; fiat money is paper money without
intrinsic value and which is not redeemable in commodity money, such
as a Federal Reserve Note. The United States started with fiat money
and quickly learned it had no value and the people refused to accept it.
During the Revolutionary War, paper fiat money—called "Continental
dollars"—was printed to finance the war. These were quickly refused
by the people who accepted them at only 10 percent of their face value,
making them so worthless that "in late-eighteenth-century America,
something of minimal value was often described as being 'not worth a
continental.' . . . It had occurred to the colonists that, as their revolution was costing quite a bit to maintain, they could go into 'temporary'
debt to finance the war. Soon it became clear that the debt could not
be repaid. Also, the printing of paper banknotes resulted in inflation.
The solution? Print more of them. Further devaluation of the continental motivated the colonists to print more. . . . The continental became
worthless, either for local trade or for repayment of debt."[6]

CHAPTER NINE

After this experience with fiat money, our Founding Fathers created a monetary system that was based upon specie, or commodity money, of gold and silver, with coins minted in each metal based on the value of the coin. Paper money that was issued was not a *note* but *legal tender*, which was redeemable in gold or silver by the US treasury. This was another check on the government provided by the Constitution. A clause in the new Constitution assured that this would never happen again by only permitting gold and silver coins to be used as tender in payment of debts. In 1792, the Coinage Act was passed which authorized three gold coins to be minted: $10.00 eagles, $5.00 half eagles, and $2.50 quarter eagles and some additional to silver coins.

Although Congress was given authority to establish the value of the money in gold and silver, the free market, and therefore, the people, were the real drivers of its value. Payments could also be made in gold or silver, allowing the people to switch between the metals as the price fluctuated in the market. The people, not the government, actually determined the value of the dollar, based upon the demand for the metals in the market.

In 1819, according to the Supreme Court, it is evident that "the framers of the Constitution clearly intended to create a national monetary system based on coinage and for the power to regulate that system to rest only with the [national] government."[7] "The delegates at the Constitutional Convention rejected a clause that would have given Congress the authority to issue paper money."[8]

This system worked very well until it was abandoned, and $1 in 1915 had the same purchasing power as $1 did in 1820 with no inflation at all. Once the government moved to the Federal Reserve system, and ultimately accepted Federal Reserve Notes as "legal tender," there has been almost constant inflation—which is really just the devaluing of the dollar. Paper fiat money, which is not redeemable in gold or silver, has always caused inflation in every country in which it has been tried during history, according to Milton Friedman, the Nobel Prize winning economist, in his 1994 book, *Money Mischief.* Inflation is not caused by prices going up in the market, but by the value of the dollar going down because the government has arbitrarily printed too much money. Inflation is caused by this government action, and not by the free market, which simply reacts to the lower value of the dollar by raising prices.

COMMODITIVE MONEY TO FIAT MONEY

This transition did not happen overnight. The History Channel explains what money was like during the early years of the country:

> For America's first 70 years, private entities, and not the federal government, issued paper money. Notes printed by state-chartered banks, which could be exchanged for gold and silver, were the most common form of paper currency in circulation. From the founding of the United States to the passage of the National Banking Act some 8,000 different entities issued currency, which created an unwieldy money supply and facilitated rampant counterfeiting. . . . On February 25, 1863, President Abraham Lincoln signed the National Banking Act (originally known as the National Currency Act), which for the first time in American history established the federal dollar as the sole currency of the United States. . . . By establishing a single national currency, the National Banking Act eliminated the overwhelming variety of paper money circulating throughout the country and created a system of banks chartered by the federal government rather than by the states.[9]

> As one means of financing the cost of fighting the Civil War, the federal (Union) government in 1862 began printing legal tender notes . . . not backed by specie (gold or silver) and exerted an inflationary impact on the Northern economy. . . . In early 1864 . . . the greenback dollar held a value of under 40 cents; by the end of the war in 1865, it was around 67 cents. . . . The Panic of 1873 struck in the fall and was followed by the worst depression in American history up to that time. . . . The Specie Resumption Act of 1875 . . . provided that on January 1, 1879, all greenbacks would be

redeemable at full face value [and the United States was back on the gold and silver standard].¹⁰

On June 5, 1933, the United States went off the gold standard, a monetary system in which currency is backed by gold, when Congress enacted a joint resolution nullifying the right of creditors to demand payment in gold. The United States had been on a gold standard since 1879. . . . Soon after taking office in March 1933, Roosevelt declared a nationwide bank moratorium . . . [and] forbade banks to pay out gold or to export it. . . . On April 5, 1933, Roosevelt ordered all gold coins and gold certificates . . . [to be] turned in for other money. It required all persons to deliver all gold coin, gold bullion and gold certificates owned by them to the Federal Reserve [Remember, the Federal Reserve System is a private banking cartel] . . . for the set price of $20.67 per ounce. . . . The government [took] in $300 million of gold coin and $470 million of gold certificates. [What constitutional authority did he have for this?] Two months later, a joint resolution of Congress abrogated the gold clauses in many public and private obligations that required the debtor to repay the creditor in gold dollars of the same weight and fineness as those borrowed. [Again, what constitutional authority did they have for this action?] In 1934, the government price of gold was increased to $35 per ounce, effectively increasing the gold on the Federal Reserve's balance sheets by 69 percent. This increase in assets allowed the Federal Reserve to further inflate the money supply [which causes inflation]. The government held the $35 per ounce price until . . . 1971, when President Richard Nixon announced that the United States would no longer convert dollars to gold at a fixed value, thus completely abandoning the gold standard. [Finally, by what authority?]¹¹

Consider the effect on the citizens of the United States when the government took their gold and paid them $20.67 an ounce, but then two years later established the value of gold at $35 per ounce. This action effectively cut the value of a dollar to 59 cents! "In the early

1960s, the silver supply for the nation's coinage was dwindling rapidly. As Congress and the administration debated over silver's future role in coinage, the silver market jumped 10 percent immediately, and another 30 percent by 1962. This set the stage for the complete elimination of silver from our coinage by the end of 1964. Any United States dime, quarter, half dollar, or dollar that is dated 1964 or earlier is made of 90 percent silver. In the dime series, all coins dated 1965 or later are clad coins and contain no silver at all."[12] Today, a silver quarter coined between 1932 and 1964 is worth $2.81 (as of March 4, 2016). This is usually the value used by coin dealers when selling these coins at melt value.[13] So, in terms of silver, inflation in the United States has been over 1,100 percent since 1964. In terms of the price of gold, inflation since 1933 has been 6,062 percent! Personally, I would not call our government's handling of its monetary responsibility a success since they abandoned, unconstitutionally, the gold and silver standard.

THE CREATION OF THE FEDERAL RESERVE

Originally, the Constitution established a gold *and* silver standard. Gold or silver could be used in payment of debts; thereby providing a check and balance within the financial system of the country. If the price of gold went up out of proportion to silver, because of scarceness, or because someone cornered the market on it, silver could be used instead. It was thought that with the vastness of the western lands, the price of silver would remain fairly stable because it was more plentiful. If the demand rose, then the price would rise, more would be found to satisfy the demand, and the price would be stabilized.

THOMAS JEFFERSON

Bank-paper must be suppressed, and the circulating medium must be restored to the nation to whom it belongs.[14]

The modern theory of the perpetuation of debt has drenched the earth with blood, and crushed its inhabitants under burdens ever accumulating.[15]

CHAPTER NINE

JAMES MADISON

> History records that the money changers have used every form of abuse, intrigue, deceit, and violent means possible to maintain their control over governments by controlling the money and its issuance.[16]

ANDREW JACKSON

> It is maintained by some that the bank is a means of executing the constitutional power "to coin money and regulate the value thereof." Congress have established a mint to coin money and passed laws to regulate the value thereof. The money so coined, with its value so regulated, and such foreign coins as Congress may adopt are the only currency known to the Constitution. But if they have other power to regulate the currency, it was conferred to be exercised by themselves, and not to be transferred to a corporation. If the bank be established for that purpose, with a charter unalterable without its consent, Congress have parted with their power for a term of years, during which the Constitution is a dead letter. It is neither necessary nor proper to transfer its legislative power to such a bank, and therefore unconstitutional.[17]

> The issue of currency is fundamentally a Government function and the system should have as basic principles soundness and elasticity. The control should be lodged with the Government and should be protected from domination or manipulation by Wall Street or any special interest. We are opposed to . . . provisions [which] would place our currency and credit system in private hands.[18]

WOODROW WILSON, YEARS AFTER SIGNING THE FEDERAL RESERVE ACT

> I am a most unhappy man. I have unwittingly ruined my country. A great industrial nation is controlled by its system of credit. Our system of credit is concentrated. The growth of the nation, therefore, and all our activities are in the hands of a few men. We

have come to be one of the worst ruled, one of the most completely controlled and dominated governments in the civilized world—no longer a government by free opinion, no longer a government by conviction and the vote of the majority, but a government by the opinion and duress of a small group of dominant men.[19]

FRANKLIN D. ROOSEVELT

The real truth of the matter is, as you and I know, that a financial element in the larger centers has owned the government ever since the days of Andrew Jackson.[20]

JAMES MADISON

The extension of the prohibition to bills of credit must give pleasure to every citizen, in proportion to his love of justice and his knowledge of the true springs of public prosperity. The loss which America has sustained since the peace, from the pestilent effects of paper money on the necessary confidence between man and man, on the necessary confidence in the public councils, on the industry and morals of the people, and on the character of republican government, constitutes an enormous debt against the States chargeable with this unadvised measure, which must long remain unsatisfied; or rather an accumulation of guilt, which can be expiated no otherwise than by a voluntary sacrifice on the altar of justice, of the power which has been the instrument of it.[21]

In 1913, the Congress of the United States created the Federal Reserve System. This act removed from Congress, and therefore, the people, the right to a fixed gold *and* silver standard whose value was established by Congress. Each coin had the intrinsic value of the metal of which it was minted. Each piece of paper money had the guarantee of the US government that it could be exchanged for hard currency made of gold or silver. Congress was given the power, and right, to fix the value of money, by passing a law defining the price of an ounce of gold and silver; and also the power to coin and print money. No one else was given the power by the Constitution to print money: therefore, there is no constitutional authority for the Federal Reserve System to print money. This system was created in direct violation of Article I of the Constitution, which states: "No state shall . . . make anything but gold and silver coin a tender in payment of debts."[22] How were the states to comply with this provision if the federal government no longer provided gold and silver as legal tender. Article I also says: "The Congress shall have power . . . to coin money [and] regulate the value thereof."[23] The Constitution does *not* authorize any *other* organization to coin money—and only a constitutional amendment can change this; no such amendment has ever been passed or even proposed.

> The few who understand the system [of cheque, money, and credits] will either be so interested in its profits, or so dependent on its favours, that there will be no opposition from that class, while on the other hand, the great body of people, mentally incapable of comprehending the tremendous advantage that capital derives from the system, will bear its burdens without complaint, and perhaps without even suspecting that the system is inimical [contrary] to their interests.[24]

THOMAS JEFFERSON

> The eyes of our citizens are not sufficiently open to the true cause of our distress. They ascribe them to everything but their true cause, the banking system; a system which if it could do good in any form, is yet so certain of leading to abuse, as to be utterly incompatible with the public safety and majority, at present all is confusion, uncertain Constitution.[25]

JOHN ADAMS

> All the perplexities, confusions, and distresses in America arise, not from defects in their Constitution or confederation, not from want of honor or virtue, so much as from downright ignorance of the nature of coin, credit, and circulation.[26]

JAMES MADISON

> Another effect of public instability is the unreasonable advantage it gives to the sagacious, the enterprising, and the moneyed few over the industrious and uninformed mass of the people.[27]

For some reason, Americans were convinced in 1913 that the control of the economy needed to be turned over to the "experts" and that the system of free enterprise, the system that had built this country, was no longer to be trusted. You may say, "Yes, but what about the tremendous changes associated with the Industrial Revolution? Things were different." Well, yes, and no. Of course things were different. Technology has changed. But has human nature changed? Has human nature ever changed? The invisible hand of the free enterprise system would work today just as it had for two hundred years prior to this century. Adam Smith was correct, and the Founding Fathers recognized it. The Founders felt the government had a responsibility to ensure a fair and level playing field, but little more, for business. The economy would regulate itself as individuals went out and voted *each and every day* when they reached into their pockets to spend their money.

The following people were behind the creation of the Federal Reserve System in 1913: Theodore Roosevelt, Paul Wasburg (representing the Rothschilds), Woodrow Wilson, Nelson W. Aldrich (representative of the Rockefellers), Frank A. Vanderlip (representative of the Rockefellers), John D. Rockefeller, Henry Davison (representative of J.P. Morgan), and Charles Norton (representative of J.P. Morgan). These proponents of the Federal Reserve System promised that it would provide society with the following benefits: (1) the steady growth of the economy by regulating economic swings between boom and bust as it controlled the amount of money available to business; (2) a way to maintain the value of the dollar—even though this had not been an issue for one hundred years; and (3) the control of interest rates on borrowed money, keeping them to 4 percent. However, none of these lofty goals have been realized. What actually happened was (1) the United States of America experienced the greatest swing in the economy within twenty years of the enactment of the Federal Reserve System—the Great Depression with the *lowest* unemployment rate of 14.3 percent for ten years; (2) the value of the dollar, in actual purchasing power, dropped from ten loaves of bread in 1913, to a quarter of a loaf in 2016; and (3) interest rates on mortgages fluctuated up to a high of 18.45 percent in 1981.[28] As you can see, this is not the track record of success: depression, recessions, the dollar worth being one tenth of what it was, and interest rates 200 to 400 percent higher than promised.

JOHN MAYNARD KEYNES

> By a continuing process of inflation, governments can confiscate, secretly and unobserved, an important part of the wealth of their citizens. . . . There is no subtler, no surer means of overturning the existing basis of society than to debauch the currency. The process engages all the hidden forces of economic law on the side of destruction, and does it in a manner which not one man in a million is able to diagnose.[29]

> John F. Kennedy had the foresight to realize what a bad deal had been struck in the creation of the Federal Reserve. He [also] had the courage to do something about it, which [unfortunately] may have cost him his life. . . . On June 4, 1963, Kennedy signed a Presidential decree, Executive Order 11110. This order virtually stripped the Federal Reserve Bank of its power to loan money to the United States Government at interest. President Kennedy declared that the privately owned Federal Reserve Bank would soon be out of business. This order gave the Treasury Department the authority to issue silver certificates against any silver in the treasury. This executive order still stands today. In less than five months after signing that executive order, President Kennedy was assassinated on November 22, 1963.[30]

I personally find his death interesting; all criminal investigative TV shows and movies say to "follow the money."

JOHN C. CALHOUN

> A power has risen up in the Government greater than the people themselves, consisting of many, and various, and powerful interests, combined into one mass, and held together by the cohesive power of the vast surplus in the banks.[31]

THE CREATION OF THE FEDERAL RESERVE

At its creation in 1913,

> The Federal Reserve promised to operate entirely under the direction and control of the President and his appointees to the Board of Governors. The Fed escaped from this control almost immediately. It has so much influence in Congress that over two hundred amendments were added to the original act, and these gradually altered the entire statutory profile of the act. Even the Secretary of the Treasury and the [Comptroller] of Currency were eliminated from its Board of Governors. Hundreds of times the Fed has defiantly acted against the interests of the American people and made billion dollar decisions favorable to its banker stockholders. In these cases, the President and the Congress found themselves helpless and unable to intervene. The former [chair] of the Federal Reserve Board, Marriner S. Eccles, admitted this to the head of the Banking and Currency Committee of the House. When Mr. Eccles was asked if the Federal Reserve had more power than either the Congress or the President, Mr. Eccles replied: "In the field of money and credit, yes."[32]

> The second deception in the whole Federal Reserve System is the fact that the private banks which own the stock in the Federal Reserve System charge the United States interest for borrowing the country's own currency![33]

The website where the previous quotes are found, should be explored further—it is very informative. What you will learn from it is that the American people have been sold worthless bills or goods, even worse than worthless; worthless would not be costing us so much in terms of interest and inflation!

Recent attempts to audit the Federal Reserve have failed. The most the bills would do is to end the ban on the Government Accountability Office's authority to audit monetary policy decisions of the Federal Reserve, and especially its open market operations and transactions with foreign central banks, which have been explicitly exempted from GAO review since 1978. Since 1947, there have been over fifty attempts to pass bills in Congress to audit the Federal Reserve; each time they have failed.[34] Personally, this is beyond my comprehension in light of the total failure of the Federal Reserve Act.

It is also worth noting that economic recessions and depressions are a naturally occurring phenomenon occurring about once every twenty years—once every generation! Consider how that would help people keep their priorities straight. Consider that in light of the purpose of our existence here on earth: Are we doing ourselves a favor by allowing government to shield us from the consequences of our own actions? How can we grow if we are? How long can government forestall the inevitable? How many more times difficult will the correction be when it occurs? Consider what has happened just within the last sixteen years!

CONCLUSION

Up to 1913, the year the Federal Reserve Act was passed, the average value, or purchasing power, of a dollar was $21.75 (in 2010 dollars), with the big fluctuations during the War of 1812 and the Civil War only. The average value of a dollar since 1913 has been $8.38 (in 2010 dollars), and has been trending downward ever since. Its value in 2015 had dropped to 91 cents.

PAUL VOLCKER, FORMER CHAIR OF THE FEDERAL RESERVE

> By now I think we can agree that the absence of an official, rules-base, cooperatively managed monetary system has not been a great success.[35]

NOTES

1. Quote attributed to Henry Ford.
2. T. Cushing Daniel, quoted in *Joint Hearings before the Subcommittees of the Committees on Banking and Currency* (Washington, D.C.: Government Printing Office, 1914), 771.
3. Alan Greenspan, "Gold and Economic Freedom," in Ayn Rand, *Capitalism: The Unknown Ideal* (New York: Signet, 1967), 96–101.
4. US Constitution, Art. I, Amend. 8.
5. US Constitution, Art. I, Amend. 10.
6. Jeff Thomas, "Not Worth a Continental," *International Man*, http://www.internationalman.com/articles/not-worth-a-continental.
7. Cecilia G. Manrique and Gabriel Manrique, "The Evolution of Virtual Currencies: Analyzing the Case of Bitcoin," in *Information and Communication Technologies in Public Administration*, ed. Christopher G. Reddick and Leonidas Anthopoulos (New York: CRC Press, 2015), 215.
8. Edward Flaherty, "A Brief History of Central Banking in the United States," *American History from Revolution to Reconstruction*, http://www.let.rug.nl/usa/essays/general/a-brief-history-of-central-banking/money-and-the-constitution.php.
9. Christopher Klein, "8 Things You May Not Know about American Money," *History Channel*, February 25, 2013, http://www.history.com/news/8-things-you-may-not-know-about-american-money.
10. "The Greenback Question," *United States History*, http://www.u-s-history.com/pages/h171.html.
11. "FDR Takes United States Off Gold Standard," *History Channel*, http://www.history.com/this-day-in-history/fdr-takes-united-states-off-gold-standard.
12. "U.S. Silver Coins: When They Ended and What They're Worth," *Coin Site*, http://coinsite.com/us-silver-coins-when-they-ended-and-what-theyre-worth/.
13. See http://www.coinflation.com/coins/1932-1964-Silver-Washington-Quarter-Value.html.
14. Letter from Thomas Jefferson to John Wayles Eppes, 1813, in *The Papers of Thomas Jefferson*, vol. 6 (Princeton: Princeton University Press), 494.
15. Ibid.
16. James Madison, quoted in David Draughon, *Financial Armageddon: The Corruption of Our Currency* (Springville, Utah: Cedar Fort, 2006), 187.

CHAPTER NINE

17. Andrew Jackson, "Message from the President of the United States, Returning the Bank Bill to the Senate with His Objections, July 10, 1832," in *Annual Messages, Veto Messages Protest, etc. of Andrew Jackson, President of the United States* (Baltimore: Edward J. Coale and Co., 1835), 236.

18. The National Progressive platform, quoted in *The American Review of Reviews: An International Magazine*, vol. 48, ed. Albert Shaw (New York: The Review of Reviews Company, July–December, 1913), 143.

19. Woodrow Wilson, quoted in Danny Schechter, *Plunder: Investigating Our Economic Calamity and the Subprime Scandal* (New York: Cosimo, 2008), 132.

20. Letter from Franklin D. Roosevelt to Colonel Edward Mandell House, November 21, 1933, as quoted in *F. D. R.: His Personal Letters, 1912–1945*, ed. Elliott Roosevelt (New York: Duell, Sloan, and Pearce, 1950), 373.

21. Federalist Papers, no. 44.

22. US Constitution, Art. I, Sec. 10.

23. US Constitution, Art. I, Sec. 8.

24. Quote attributed to Nathaniel Meyer Rothschild speech, speaking to a group of international bankers in 1912, in William Finck, *ChristReich: A Commentary on the Revelation of Yahshua Christ* (William Finck, 2009), 184; and to John Sherman, in Michael A. Kirchubel, *Vile Acts of Evil: Banking in America*, vol. 1 (Michael A. Kirchubel, 2009), 60.

25. Letter from Thomas Jefferson to Richard Rush, June 22, 1819, on Library of Congress, https://www.loc.gov/resource/mtj1.051_0635_0636/?sp=2.

26. John Adams, quoted in Leslie Snyder Bates, Why Gold?: The One Sure Cure for Inflation and Economic Tyranny (Bloomington, Indiana: AuthorHouse, 1974), xix.

27. Federalist Papers, no. 62.

28. See http://www.freddiemac.com/pmms/pmms30.htm.

29. John Maynard Keynes, quoted in N. Gregory Mankiw, *MacroEconomics*, (Worth Publishers, 2002), 101.

30. Vincent Gioia, "The Federal Reserve Bank—It's Not What You Think," *Right Side News*, December 1, 2008, http://www.rightsidenews.com/editorial/us-opinion-and-editorial/the-federal-reserve-bank-its-not-what-you-think/.

31. John C. Calhoun, *The Works of John C. Calhoun*, vol. 2 (New York: D. Appleton and Company, 1883), 568.

32. H. S. Kenan, *The Federal Reserve Bank* (Noontide Press, 1970), 206, on *National Center for Constitutional Studies*, https://nccs.net/online

-resources/the-urgent-need-for-a-comprehensive-monetary-reform/how -the-federal-reserve-system-operates-and-why-it-has-failed.

33. *National Center for Constitutional Studies*, https://nccs.net/online -resources/the-urgent-need-for-a-comprehensive-monetary-reform/how-the -federal-reserve-system-operates-and-why-it-has-failed.

34. See https://www.washingtonpost.com/news/monkey-cage/wp/2016/01/11 /a-brief-history-of-attempts-to-audit-the-fed-rand-paul-is-a-latecomer/.

35. Paul Volcker, quoted in Nathan Lewis, "A 'Rules-Based' Monetary System Means a Fixed-Value System," *Forbes*, November 19, 2014, http://www .forbes.com/sites/nathanlewis/2014/11/19/a-rules-based-monetary-system -means-a-fixed-value-system/#4260e1f84774.

TEN

The Explosive Growth in the Use and Acceptance of Executive Orders

THOMAS JEFFERSON

> The executive in our government is not the sole, it is scarcely the principal object of my jealousy. The tyranny of the legislature is the most formidable dread at present and will be for many years. That of the executive will come in its turn, but it will be at a remote period.[1]

Executive orders issued by the president, and regulations issued by regulatory agencies, being upheld *as law* by the Supreme Court is another example of the unconstitutional—that is, without ratified amendment—removal of one of the original checks and balances put into the Constitution by the Founding Fathers. Executive orders bypass Congress, and therefore the people, who have the exclusive right to make laws by common consent through their representatives as outlined in the Constitution. Article I of the Constitution says, "The Congress shall have power . . . to make *all laws* which shall be necessary and proper . . . [to carry out the enumerated powers given them in the document]."[2] No other group, or individual, is empowered to do this because no other group is directly accountable to the American people and to the states like the Congress is.

Originally, the people had direct control over their laws by being represented by those who made the laws, and the process for the creation of laws was, and still is, clearly defined in the Constitution. A law had to be passed by the House or Senate, and then approved by the majority vote of the other house, before being sent to the President for his signature. All three had to agree on its passage: the House representing the people, the Senate representing the states, and the president (a presidential veto could still be overridden by a supermajority of the House and Senate, of course) representing the country. The lawmakers were, also, immediately accountable to the people at reelection time for the laws they passed. "No taxation without representation" was the common cry of the colonists; and now we have the same problem two hundred years later with distant, unelected, unaccountable agency bureaucrats creating rules and regulations for our safety, environment, economy, businesses, families, and property. And what's more, the courts are enforcing these rules and regulations as *laws*. If they are enforced as *laws*, it does not matter what we call them, or who issues them.

Presidents have been busy executing executive orders that are being enforced as laws. There are presently *over* 13,700 executive orders on the books that are being enforced as laws.[3] A good example of one is the 55 mph speed limit imposed on the nation by President Jimmy Carter on an area that was clearly reserved to the states. The US Department of Transportation had to "blackmail" the states into enforcing it by withholding federal highway funds if it wasn't enforced. Is this what the Founders envisioned? Is this an honorable situation? This is what happens though, whenever someone tries to get something for nothing; as the states have been doing by requesting financial assistance from the national government. They got the assistance *and* the regulations that came along with it.

The president, under the Constitution, was given the authority to issue executive orders, but only during times of national emergency: such as, invasion and insurrection, or to carry out laws created by Congress. The Emancipation Proclamation was issued by President Lincoln, constitutionally, during an insurrection—and it's intent was primarily military, although it obviously was pleasing to him for moral and personal reasons. It had to be followed though, by the Thirteenth, Fourteenth, and Fifteenth Amendments to the Constitution to make it the law of the land once the national emergency had passed.

There is another principle here: be wary whenever a politician tries to make crisis proportions out of any situation. The usurpation of power has always been preceded by a "perceived" crisis. Politicians of today even joke about "never letting a serious crisis go to waste." The problem is that typically they create the crisis in the first place, and then use it to expand the powers of government without a constitutional amendment.

> In the early 1930s the Congress became nervous about delegating so much of its lawmaking power to the executive branch, and so it began monitoring the various agencies to make certain they were issuing executive orders in harmony with the original intent of Congress. However, in 1984 the Supreme Court declared that it was a violation of the separation-of-powers doctrine to have the Congress monitoring the administration of the executive branch. Amazingly, the court did not say that it was a violation of the separation-of-powers doctrine to have the Congress delegating its lawmaking powers to the executive branch in the first place.[4]

EXPONENTIAL GROWTH OF EXECUTIVE ORDERS

The number of executive orders signed by each president has increased by two orders of magnitude since George Washington. Along with executive orders, we have bureaucratic regulations that are now interpreted and accepted by the Supreme Court as law, which were not passed by Congress or accepted by the president. Keep in mind what James Madison said: "It will be of little avail to the people, that the laws are made by men of their own choice, if the laws be so voluminous that they cannot be read, or so incoherent that they cannot be understood."[5] This seems to me to describe our current situation with Federal regulations. Currently, there are 81,611 pages in the 2015

Federal Register of laws, rules, and regulations.[6] The Code of Federal Regulations (CFR) is a codification of the general and permanent rules that the executive departments and agencies of the federal government have published in the *Federal Register*. "The number of specific regulatory restrictions listed in the *Code of Federal Regulations* (CFR) topped one million in 2010. The CFR has grown by more than 42,000 pages in the last twenty years. The most recent print edition contains 174,545 thrilling pages—nearly a quarter of which have been added since the Clinton administration took office. The print edition takes up 238 volumes, and the index alone runs 1,242 pages. The number of individual regulatory restrictions in the CFR topped one million in 2010."[7] It is interesting to contrast the number of words needed by some truly great examples of writing. To illustrate this point, David McIntosh writing in the *National Review* (October 24, 1995) said, "The Lord's Prayer contains 66 words. The Gettysburg Address contains 286 words. There are 1,322 words in the Declaration of Independence. But government regulations on the sale of cabbage contains 26,911."[8]

JAMES MADISON

> The House of Representatives cannot only refuse, but they alone can propose, the supplies requisite for the support of government. They, in a word, hold the purse. . . . This power over the purse may, in fact, be regarded as the most complete and effectual weapon with which any constitution can arm the immediate representatives of the people, for obtaining a redress of every grievance, and for carrying into effect every just and salutary measure.[9]

> The internal effects of a mutable [changeable] policy are still more calamitous. It poisons the blessing of liberty itself. *It will be of little avail to the people, that the laws are made by men of their own choice, if the laws be so voluminous that they cannot be read, or so incoherent that they cannot be understood; if they be repealed or revised before they are promulgated, or undergo such incessant changes that no man, who knows what the law is to-day, can guess what it will be to-morrow. Law*

is defined to be a rule of action; but how can that be a rule, which is little known, and less fixed? . . . But the most deplorable effect of all is that diminution of attachment and reverence which steals into the hearts of the people, towards a political system which betrays so many marks of infirmity, and disappoints so many of their flattering hopes. No government, any more than an individual, will long be respected without being truly respectable; nor be truly respectable, without possessing a certain portion of order and stability.[10]

The greatest calamity to which the United States can be subject, is a vicissitude of laws, and continual shifting and changing from one object to another, which must expose the people to various inconveniences.—This has a certain effect, of which sagacious men always have, and always will make an advantage. From whom is advantage made? From the industrious farmers and tradesmen, who are ignorant of the means of making such advantages. The people will not be exposed to these inconveniences under an uniform and steady course of legislation. But they have been so heretofore.[11]

Another effect of public instability [due to changes in the law] is the unreasonable advantage it gives to the sagacious, the enterprising, and the moneyed few [who can pay others to keep up with the changes] over the industrious and uninformed mass of the people [who are simply trying to make an honest living].[12]

ALEXIS DE TOCQUEVILLE

The species of oppression by which democratic nations are menaced is unlike anything that ever before existed in the world. . . . The supreme power then extends its arm over the whole community. It covers the surface of society with a network of small complicated rules, minute and uniform, through which the most original minds and the most energetic characters cannot penetrate, to rise above the crowd. *The will of man is not shattered, but is softened, bent, and guided; men seldom are forced by it to act, but they are constantly restrained from acting. Such a power does not destroy, but it prevents existence; it does not tyrannize, but it compresses, ener- vates, extinguishes, and stupefies a people, till each nation is reduced to nothing better than a flock of timid and industrious animals, of which the government is the shepherd.*[13]

EXECUTIVE ORDERS AND WELFARE PROGRAMS

Now that the national government has become involved with welfare programs, we can see how inefficient it is for government to provide these programs. A study of government income distribution programs versus private charities concluded:

[Government] income redistribution agencies are estimated to absorb about two-thirds of each dollar budgeted to them in over- head costs, and in some cases as much as three-quarters of each dollar. Using government data, Robert L. Woodson . . . calculated that, on average, 70 cents of each dollar budgeted for government assistance goes not to the poor, but to the members of the welfare bureaucracy and others serving the poor. Michael Tanner . . . cites regional studies supporting this 70/30 split. In contrast, admin- istrative and other operating costs in private charities absorb, on average, only one-third or less of each dollar donated, leaving the other two-thirds (or more) to be delivered to recipients. Charity Navigator (www.charitynavigator.org), the newest of several private sector organizations that rate charities by various criteria and supply that information to the public on their web sites, found that, as of 2004, 70 percent of charities they rated spent at least 75 percent of their budgets on the programs and services they exist to provide, and 90 percent spent at least 65 percent. The median administrative expense among all charities in their sample was only 10.3 percent. . . . In fact, the average cost of private charity generally is almost certainly *lower* than the one-quarter to one-third estimated by Charity Navigator and other private sector charity rating services.[14]

CHAPTER TEN

One commentator has asked, "How is it that after more than 40 years since the Great Society and more than $8 trillion spent (in 2000 dollars) so little headway has been made by the government in alleviating poverty?" He then answered the question,

> Observing the English Poor Laws in 1835, Alexis de Tocqueville wrote in *Memoirs on Pauperism*: "Man, like all socially-organized beings, has a natural passion for idleness. There are, however, two incentives to work: the need to live and the desire to improve conditions of life." In effect, the government destroys both of these incentives. By receiving food, shelter, and most other necessities, welfare recipients aren't faced with the need to provide for themselves. Likewise, by supporting all lifestyle decisions, both good and bad, government insulates the poor from having to face the consequences of unfavorable choices. Tocqueville was prescient in his critique of government welfare, forecasting, "I have said that the inevitable result of public charity was to perpetuate idleness among the majority of the poor and to provide for their leisure at the expense of those who work." By traditionally allocating the bulk of its resources as cash payments, the government increased dependency and neglected to address the causes of perpetual poverty.[15]

NOTES

1. Letter from Thomas Jefferson to James Madison, March 15, 1789.
2. US Constitution, Art. I, Sec. 8; emphasis added.
3. See http://www.archives.gov/federal-register/executive-orders/disposition .html.
4. W. Cleon Skousen, *The Making of America: The Substance and Meaning of the Constitution* (Washington, D.C.: The National Center for Constitutional Studies, 1985), 254–55.
5. Federalist Papers, no. 62.
6. See Alex Swoyer, "2015 Sets Regulation Record: Federal Register Hits All Time High 81,611 Pages," *Breitbart*, December 30, 2015, http://www .breitbart.com/big-government/2015/12/30/2015-sets-regulation-record -federal-register-hits-time-high-81611-pages/.

7. Clyde Wayne Crews and Ryan Young, "Twenty Years of Non-Stop Regulation," *The American Spectator*, June 5, 2013, http://spectator.org /articles/55475/twenty-years-non-stop-regulation.

8. Quoted in Keith B. Willis, "Phantom Cabbage Regulation," *The Washington Post*, September 2, 1995, https://www.englishclub.com/ref/esl/Quotes /Government/The_Lord_s_Prayer_is_66_words..._2748.htm.

9. Federalist Papers, no. 58.

10. Federalist Papers, no. 62; emphasis added.

11. James Madison, in *The Debates, Resolutions, and Other Proceedings, in Convention, on the Adoption of the Federal Constitution, as Recommended by the General Convention at Philadelphia*, comp., Jonathan Elliot (Washington, D.C.: Jonathan Elliot, 1828), 206.

12. Federalist Papers, no. 62.

13. Alexis de Tocqueville, *Democracy in America*, vol. 2, trans., Henry Reeve (Project Gutenberg, 2006); emphasis added.

14. James Rolph Edwards, "The Costs of Public Income Redistribution and Private Charity," *Journal of Libertarian Studies* 21, no. 2 (summer 2007); emphasis added.

15. Jude Blanchette, "The Shortcomings of Government Charity," *Foundation for Economic Education*, May 1, 2007, http://fee.org/articles /the-shortcomings-of-government-charity/.

ELEVEN

The Lost Understanding of the Original Intent of the Second Amendment

S tudies indicate that firearms are used over two million times a year for personal protection, and that the presence of a firearm, without a shot being fired, prevents crime in many instances. Shooting usually can be justified only where crime constitutes an immediate imminent threat to life, limb, or in some cases, property."[1]

PATRICK HENRY

If I am asked what is to be done when a people feel themselves intolerably oppressed, my answer is ready—overturn the government. But do not, I beseech you, carry matters to this length without provocation. Wait, at least, until some infringement is made upon your rights, and which cannot otherwise be redressed.[2]

BENJAMIN FRANKLIN

Rebellion to tyrants is obedience to God.[3]

THOMAS JEFFERSON

The spirit of resistance to government is so valuable on certain occasions, that I wish it to be always kept alive. It will often be exercised when wrong, but better so than not to be exercised at all. I like a little rebellion now and then. It is like a storm in the atmosphere.[4]

DANIEL WEBSTER

God grants liberty only to those who love it, and are always ready to guard and defend it.[5]

When a person is so afraid of a gun that he or she demonizes guns or people with guns, they are showing the primary sign of hoplophobia. "Imagining guns or gun owners to all have evil moral characteristics could readily lead to hoplophobia. . . . Demonization is most successful, politically speaking, when it induces in the general public a 'moral panic'—defining of a group of people or a certain behavior as a threat to social values. In a moral panic, the media presents persons, objects, or activities in a stereotyped and hysterical fashion, urging that immediate action be taken, without time for reflection. A moral panic is often set off by an 'atrocity tale,' which is an event (real or imaginary) that evokes moral outrage, implicitly justifies punitive actions against those considered responsible for the event, and mobilizes society to control the perpetrators."[6] Unfortunately, this is the situation in which we find ourselves in twenty-first-century America.

This was not always the case, and it seems to be a symptom of urbanization. When the population was primarily living on farms, and using guns like any other tool, there was no fear of them or the persons possessing them. As the need for a gun diminished in American society, they were seen, handled, and used less frequently and they have been given this anthropomorphic characterization as being evil. This feeling, because it is not a rational thought, needs to be evaluated because there may be an important need for firearms in the hands of everyday citizens in our society. The Founding Fathers definitely believed there was, and not just because they were primarily farmers. So, what can this legitimate purpose be? The Founding Fathers provided the answer in the Declaration of Independence:

CHAPTER ELEVEN

We hold these truths to be self-evident, that all men are created equal, that they are endowed by their Creator with certain unalienable Rights, that among these are Life, Liberty and the pursuit of Happiness. That to secure these rights, Governments are instituted among Men, deriving their just powers from the consent of the governed. That whenever any Form of Government becomes destructive of these ends, it is the Right of the People to alter or to abolish it, and to institute new Government, laying its foundation on such principles and organizing its powers in such form, as to them shall seem most likely to effect their Safety and Happiness. Prudence, indeed, will dictate that Governments long established should not be changed for light and transient causes; and accordingly all experience hath shown that mankind are more disposed to suffer, while evils are sufferable, than to right themselves by abolishing the forms to which they are accustomed. *But when a long train of abuses and usurpations, pursuing invariably the same Object evinces [shows plainly] a design to reduce them under absolute Despotism, it is their right, it is their duty, to throw off such Government, and to provide new Guards for their future security.*[7]

How is this to occur? Through wishful thinking? Or better yet, we'll just ask the tyrants to give up their power! President Joseph Fielding Smith says, "Now I tell you it is time the people of the United States were waking up with the understanding that if they don't save the Constitution from the dangers that threaten it, we will have a change of government."[8] And President Ezra Taft Benson says, "Once freedom is lost, only blood—human blood—will win it back. There are some things we can and must do at once if we are to stave off a holocaust of destruction. *First:* We must return to worship the God of this land, who is Jesus Christ. . . . *Second:* We must *awaken to 'a sense of [our] awful situation*, because of this secret combination which [is] among [us]'* (Ether 8:24)."[9]

SECRET COMBINATIONS

In the previous quote, President Benson referred to chapter 8 in the book of Ether.

> 24 Wherefore, the Lord commandeth you, when ye shall see these things come among you that ye shall awake to a sense of your awful situation, because of this secret combination which shall be among you; or wo be unto it, because of the blood of them who have been slain; for they cry from the dust for vengeance upon it, and also upon those who built it up.
>
> 25 For it cometh to pass that whoso buildeth it up seeketh to overthrow the freedom of all lands, nations, and countries; and it bringeth to pass the destruction of all people, for it is built up by the devil, who is the father of all lies; even that same liar who beguiled our first parents, yea, even that same liar who hath caused man to commit murder from the beginning; who hath hardened the hearts of men that they have murdered the prophets, and stoned them, and cast them out from the beginning. (Ether 8:24–25)

How is it that these secret combinations, such as those of the Gadianton robbers, work? This is what Nephi, son of Helaman, had to say:

> 4 And seeing the people in a state of such awful wickedness, and those Gadianton robbers filling the judgment-seats—having usurped the power and authority of the land; laying aside the commandments of God, and not in the least aright before him; doing no justice unto the children of men;
>
> 5 Condemning the righteous because of their righteousness; letting the guilty and the wicked go unpunished because of their money; and moreover to be held in office at the head of government, to rule and do according to their wills, that they might get gain and glory of the world, and, moreover, that they might the more easily commit adultery, and steal, and kill, and do according to their own wills—

6 Now this great iniquity had come upon the Nephites, in the space of not many years; and when Nephi saw it, his heart was swollen with sorrow within his breast. (Helaman 7:4–6)

Moroni explains further:

9 Behold, is there not an account concerning them of old, that they by *their secret plans did obtain kingdoms and great glory?*

13 And it came to pass that Akish gathered in unto the house of Jared all his kinsfolk, and said unto them: Will ye swear unto me that ye will be faithful unto me in the thing which I shall desire of you?

14 And it came to pass that *they all sware unto him*, by the God of heaven, and also by the heavens, and also by the earth, and by their heads, *that whoso should vary from the assistance which Akish desired should lose his head; and whoso should divulge whatsoever thing Akish made known unto them, the same should lose his life.*

15 And it came to pass that thus they did agree with Akish. And Akish did administer unto them the oaths which were given by them of old *who also sought power*, which had been handed down even from Cain, who was a murderer from the beginning.

16 And they were kept up by the power of the devil to administer these oaths . . . to keep them in darkness, *to help such as sought power to gain power, and to murder, and to plunder, and to lie*, and to commit all manner of wickedness and whoredoms.

18 And it came to pass that they formed a secret combination, even as they of old; which combination *is most abominable and wicked above all*, in the sight of God.

20 And now I, Moroni, do not write the manner of their oaths and combinations, for it hath been made known unto me *that they are had among all people. . . .*

21 And they have caused the destruction of this people of whom I am now speaking, and also the destruction of the people of Nephi.

22 *And whatsoever nation shall uphold such secret combinations, to get power and gain, until they shall spread over the nation, behold,*

they shall be destroyed; for the Lord will not suffer that the blood of his saints, which shall be shed by them, shall always cry unto him from the ground for vengeance upon them and yet he avenge them not.

23 Wherefore, O ye Gentiles [us in America], it is wisdom in God that these things should be shown unto you, that thereby ye may repent of your sins, and *suffer not that these murderous combinations shall get above you, which are built up to get power and gain*—and the work, yea, even the work of destruction come upon you, yea, even the sword of the justice of the Eternal God shall fall upon you, to your overthrow and destruction if ye shall suffer these things to be.

24 Wherefore, the Lord commandeth you, when ye shall see these things come among you that ye shall awake to a sense of your awful situation, because of this secret combination which shall be among you; or wo be unto it, because of the blood of them who have been slain; for they cry from the dust for vengeance upon it, and also upon those who built it up.

25 For it cometh to pass that whoso buildeth it up seeketh to overthrow the freedom of all lands, nations, and countries; and it bringeth to pass the destruction of all people, for it is built up by the devil, who is the father of all lies; even that same liar who beguiled our first parents, yea, even that same liar who hath caused man to commit murder from the beginning; who hath hardened the hearts of men that they have murdered the prophets, and stoned them, and cast them out from the beginning.

26 Wherefore, I, Moroni, am commanded to write these things. (Ether 8:9, 13–16, 18, 20–26; emphasis added)

For whom were these things written? To what people, and at what time in history? Chapter 13 in 1 Nephi tells us:

30 Nevertheless, thou beholdest that the Gentiles who have gone forth out of captivity, and have been lifted up by the power of God above all other nations, upon the face of the land which is choice above all other lands, which is the land that the Lord God hath

covenanted with thy father that his seed should have for the land of their inheritance. (1 Nephi 13:30)

There is obviously a secondary purpose to the Book of Mormon, which is to warn Americans, in the latter days when the Book of Mormon comes forth, of their awful situation when a secret combination will be in place to destroy our freedom. If we evaluate the three God-given rights referenced in the Declaration of Independence, and more clearly defined in section 134 of the Doctrine and Covenants, we have to conclude that it is actually one right—the right to use lethal force—to protect the three rights defined: life, liberty, and property. Without the ability to protect each of these, the rights are unenforceable and meaningless. This is true regarding government as well, if we, the citizens do not maintain for ourselves the ability to overthrow our own government when it becomes necessary, as stated in the Declaration of Independence: "When a long train of abuses and usurpations, pursuing invariably the same object evinces a design to reduce them under absolute despotism, it is their right, it is their duty, to throw off such government, and to provide new guards for their future security."[10] This is what it means to be a "citizen," who is sovereign and has created government to protect his rights, versus a "subject."

THOMAS JEFFERSON

What country before ever existed a century and half without a rebellion? And what country can preserve its liberties if their rulers are not warned from time to time that their people preserve the spirit of resistance? Let them take arms. The remedy is to set them right as to facts, pardon and pacify them. What signifies a few lives lost in a century or two? The tree of liberty must be refreshed from time to time with the blood of patriots and tyrants.[11]

JAMES MADISON

The amendments which have occurred to me, proper to be recommended by Congress to the State Legislatures, are these: First. That there be prefixed to the Constitution a declaration, that all power is originally vested in, and consequently derived from, the people. That government is instituted and ought to be exercised for the benefit of the people, which consists in the enjoyment of life and liberty, with the right of acquiring and using property, and generally of pursuing and obtaining happiness and safety. That the People have an indubitable, unalienable, and indefeasible right to reform or change their Government, whenever it be found adverse or inadequate to the purposes of its institution.[12]

It will not be denied, that power is of an encroaching nature, and that it ought to be effectually restrained from passing the limits assigned to it. . . . The legislative department is everywhere extending the sphere of its activity, and drawing all power into its impetuous vortex. . . . The conclusion which I am warranted in drawing from these observations is, that a mere demarcation on parchment of the constitutional limits of the several departments, is not a sufficient guard against those encroachments which lead to a tyrannical concentration of all the powers of government in the same hands.[13]

PATRICK HENRY

If we wish to be free, if we mean to preserve inviolate those inestimable privileges for which we have been so long contending, if we mean not basely to abandon the noble struggle in which we have been so long engaged, and which we have pledged ourselves never to abandon until the glorious object of our contest shall be obtained, we must fight! I repeat it, sir, we must fight! An appeal to arms and to the God of Hosts is all that is left us![14]

Where is this spirit in America today? There is no longer found in America a well-accepted and clearly understood respect for "the right of the people to keep and bear arms,"[15] for the purpose of fighting their own government *if* it becomes necessary. The Founders recognized that this right of the individual citizens was "essential" for the preservation of liberty. This was to be organized and lead by the States using their militias consisting of the people with their own military-style weapons.

CHAPTER ELEVEN

The Militia Act of 1903—together with its 1908 amendment . . . repealed the Militia Act of 1792 and divided the militia into two groups: the Reserve Militia, defined as all able-bodied men between 18 and 45, and the Organized Militia, defined as state units receiving federal support. . . . The act gave the President the power to call the Organized Militia—that is, the National Guard—into federal service for up to nine months' service to repel invasion, suppress rebellion, or enforce federal laws, *but not for service outside the United States*. Guardsmen had to answer a presidential call or face court-martial, and states had to organize, equip, and train their units in accordance with the organization, standards, and procedures of the Regular Army. . . . In 1908 the act was amended. The nine-month limit on federal service was deleted; the President would now set the length of federal service. The ban on Guard units serving outside the United States was dropped. Clearly establishing the Guard's role as the Army's reserve force, the amended act stated that during a mobilization the Guard had to be called before the Army could organize a federal volunteer force. . . . Congress later in 1916 passed the National Defense Act. This law . . . determin[ed] the Guard's role in national defense and assert[ed] federal control over state military forces. . . . In addition, the War Department could now dictate the number and types of a state Guard's units and could impose uniform enlistment contracts and standards for commissions in the Guard. Guardsmen had to take both state and federal oaths and could be drafted into federal service. . . . The Guard had lost most of its autonomy and much of its fraternal character so prized by state soldiers.[16]

All of this undermined one of the primary reasons for the militia being under state control—to be used to effectively thwart the national government through an appeal to arms.

The Founding Fathers feared a standing army. They had direct experience with the British Army during the colonial period, and they did not like it! Hence, the Second Amendment creating state militias, and the Third Amendment: "No soldier shall, in time of peace be quartered in any house, without the consent of the owner, nor in time of war, but in a manner to be prescribed by law."[17]

ALEXANDER HAMILTON

> Yet it is a matter of the utmost importance that a well-digested plan should, as soon as possible, be adopted for the proper establishment of the militia. . . . It will be possible to have an excellent body of well-trained militia, ready to take the field whenever the defense of the State shall require it. This will not only lessen the call for military establishments, but if circumstances should at any time oblige the government to form an army of any magnitude that army can never be formidable to the liberties of the people while there is a large body of citizens, little, if at all, inferior to them in discipline and the use of arms, who stand ready to defend their own rights and those of their fellow-citizens. This appears to me the only substitute that can be devised for a standing army, and the best possible security against it, if it should exist. . . . If there should be [a standing] army to be made use of as the engine of despotism, what need of the militia? If there should be no army . . . would the militia, irritated by being called upon to undertake a distant and hopeless expedition, for the purpose of riveting the chains of slavery upon a part of their countrymen, direct their course, but to the seat of the tyrants, . . . to crush them in their imagined entrenchments of power, and to make them an example of the just vengeance of an abused and incensed people? . . . If we were even to suppose the national rulers actuated by the most ungovernable ambition, it is impossible to believe that they would employ such preposterous means to accomplish their designs.[18]

JAMES MADISON

> Let a regular army, fully equal to the resources of the country, be formed; and let it be entirely at the devotion of the federal government; still it would not be going too far to say, that the State

governments, with the people on their side, would be able to repel the danger . . . a standing army . . . carried in any country, does not exceed one hundredth part of the whole number of souls; or one twenty-fifth part of the number able to bear arms. . . . To these would be opposed a militia . . . officered by men chosen from among themselves, fighting for their common liberties, and united and conducted by [state] governments possessing their affections and confidence. It may well be doubted, whether a militia thus circumstanced could ever be conquered by such a proportion of regular troops. . . . Besides the advantage of being armed, which the Americans possess over the people of almost every other nation, the existence of subordinate governments, to which the people are attached, and by which the militia officers are appointed, forms a barrier against the enterprises of ambition, more insurmountable than any which a simple government of any form can admit of. . . . The several kingdoms of Europe . . . are afraid to trust the people with arms. . . . It may be affirmed with the greatest assurance, that the throne of every tyranny in Europe would be speedily overturned in spite of the legions which surround it. Let us not insult the free and gallant citizens of America with the suspicion, that they would be less able to defend the rights of which they would be in actual possession. . . . Let us rather no longer insult.[19]

THOMAS JEFFERSON

Standing armies [are] inconsistent with [a people's] freedom and subversive of their quiet.[20]

Bonaparte . . . transferred the destinies of the republic from the civil to the military arm. Some will use this as a lesson against the practicability of republican government. I read it as a lesson against the danger of standing armies.[21]

The Greeks and Romans had no standing armies, yet they defended themselves. The Greeks by their laws, and the Romans by the spirit of their people, took care to put into the hands of their rulers no such engine of oppression, as a standing army. Their system was to make every man a soldier, and oblige him to repair to the standard of his country, whenever that was reared. This made them invincible; and the same remedy will make us so.[22]

Our duty is . . . to act upon things as they are and to make a reasonable provision for whatever they may be. Were armies to be raised whenever a speck of war is visible in our horizon, we never should have been without them. Our resources would have been exhausted on dangers which have never happened, instead of being reserved for what is really to take place.[23]

Notice in the Second Amendment that the word "arms" was the most generic, all-inclusive word that could have been chosen. It didn't restrict pistols, or any "new technology" that the Founders knew about. Consider this in light of the following quotations. Why are we now then restricting (1) automatic weapons, (2) pistols, and (3) semi-automatic weapons as if one type of weapon is any more dangerous than any other type. The Founders felt that the right of the individual to "keep and bear arms" was the bulwark of the republic, and a necessity if we were to fight a standing army.

The constitutional protection found in the Bill of Rights for the freedom to worship, the freedoms of speech and press, the right to assemble, and the right to petition, and so on, are possible, over the long haul, only because of the Second Amendment; the right of *the people* to keep and bear arms; which is the keystone of all the other rights guaranteed. The people are sovereign only as long as they are respected as such by their leaders. This happens, historically, only if they maintain for themselves the power to "throw off such government, and to provide new guards for their future security" as Thomas Jefferson wrote for the Founding Fathers in the Declaration of Independence. Please, note that the same document calls it "their right, . . . their duty" to do this. We have this inalienable, God-given right. Inalienable rights supercede constitutional rights, which simply define how we will be treated by government during any legal action against us.

As Mark Levin recognized in 2012, "We're already living in a post-Constitutional America."[24] Our inalienable rights have been ignored by the courts, and our constitutional rights have been undermined or eliminated by the War on Poverty (property rights), the War on Drugs (privacy rights), and the War on Terror (right to life, liberty, and property without due process). Currently, contrary to the Fourth Amendment of the Bill of Rights, National Security Letters (NSLs) are issued by FBI agents, without a judge's approval, to obtain personal information on citizens, and there is no requirement to destroy the information obtained even if the citizen is determined to be innocent. Over 34,000 law enforcement and intelligence agents have access to phone records acquired through NSLs. And the "Patriot" Act prohibits citizens who receive NSLs from telling anyone. During just two years (2003 to 2005) only fifty-three cases were referred to prosecutors as a result of over 143,000 NSLs—and none of them were for terrorism.[25]

The philosophy of the Founding Fathers can be summarized in one simple yet powerful statement: An armed man is a *citizen*; and an unarmed man is a *subject*. Citizens have inalienable rights while subjects only have privileges granted to them by the government.

THOMAS JEFFERSON

No freeman shall ever be debarred the use of arms.[26]

Laws that forbid the carrying of arms . . . disarm only those who are neither inclined nor determined to commit crimes. Such laws make things worse for the assaulted and better for the assailants; they serve rather to encourage than prevent homicides, for an unarmed man may be attacked with greater confidence than an armed man.[27]

JAMES MADISON

"The ultimate authority . . . resides in the people alone," and predicted that encroachments on individual freedoms would provoke "plans of resistance" and an "appeal to a trial of force." . . . The advantage of being armed, . . . the Americans possess over the people of almost every other nation. . . . Notwithstanding the military establishments in the several kingdoms of Europe, which are carried as far as the public resources will bear, the governments are afraid to trust the people with arms.[28]

The right of the people to keep and bear arms shall not be infringed; a well armed, and well regulated militia being the best security of a free country.[29]

PATRICK HENRY

Guard with jealous attention the public liberty. Suspect everyone who approaches that jewel. Unfortunately, nothing will preserve it but downright force. Whenever you give up that force, you are inevitably ruined.[30]

RICHARD HENRY LEE

To preserve liberty, it is essential that the whole body of the people always possess arms, and be taught alike, especially when young, how to use them.[31]

SAMUEL ADAMS

And that the said Constitution be never construed to authorize Congress to . . . prevent the people of the United States, who are peaceable citizens, from keeping their own arms.[32]

GEORGE WASHINGTON

A free people ought not only to be armed, but disciplined.[33] [In reference to state militias.]

That no man should scruple, or hesitate a moment to use a-ms [arms] in defence of so valuable a blessing [as liberty], on which all the good and evil of life depends; is clearly my opinion; Yet A-ms [arms] . . . should be the last . . . resource.[34]

CHAPTER ELEVEN

NORTH CAROLINA RATIFYING CONVENTION

> That Government ought to be instituted for the common benefit, protection and security, of the people; and that the doctrine of non-resistance against arbitrary, power and oppression is absurd, slavish, and destructive to the good and happiness of mankind.[35]

ALEXANDER HAMILTON

> If the representatives of the people betray their constituents [by usurping power], there is then no resource left but in the exertion of that original right of self-defence which is paramount to all positive forms of government.[36]

JAMES OTIS

> And he that would palm the doctrine of unlimited passive obedience and non-resistance upon mankind, . . . is not only a fool and a knave, but a rebel against common sense, as well as the laws of God, of Nature, and his Country.[37]

GEORGE MASON

> To disarm the people [is] the best and most effectual way to enslave them.[38]

THE FAILURE OF THE STATE TO PROTECT

One of the greatest contradictions in our present society is that while our legislatures are enacting one "gun control" measure after another to restrict our access to firearms, the courts have consistently ruled that it is *not* the responsibility of the government, through police departments, to protect the individual citizen. In my former state of Maryland, I had to have documented police reports supporting my claim that someone was trying to kill me in order to exercise my inalienable right to "bear arms" and get a permit to carry a pistol. My *right* had been turned into a *privilege* that was regulated and revoked by the state. Curious when compared to the Founders philosophy that government is the creation of the people to protect their individual rights.

THE US COURT OF APPEALS, 1982

There is no constitutional right to be protected *by the state* against being murdered by criminals or madmen. It is monstrous if the state fails to protect its residents against such predators, but it does not violate the due process clause of the Fourteenth Amendment or, we suppose, any other provision of the Constitution. The Constitution is a charter of negative liberties; it tells the state to let people alone; it does not require the federal government or the state to provide services, even so elementary a service as maintaining law and order.[39]

According to Bob Scully, President of the National Association of Police Organizations, (Washington, D.C.) in a letter received by the author on March 24, 1993:

Crime does pay! I know it and so does every murderer, rapist, and robber on your block! They know there's a darn good chance they won't do time for rape. And they won't get the death penalty for murder . . . there's one opportunity they will get . . . the chance to hurt another innocent citizen . . .—or even an innocent child. . . . Consider the horrifying statistics: (1) in some big cities, only one serious crime in one hundred leads to anyone doing time; (2) the average sentence for burglary is just 5.4 days; (3) the average sentence for car theft is only 3.8 days; and (4) the average sentence a murderer might serve for a killing is only 2.3 years. The review of the FBI's UCR statistics dating back to 1995 is interesting. It shows that over those years, Part 1 crimes decreased by nearly three millions incidents. This is significant especially when you combine that with a 19 percent increase in the U.S. population during that same period of time. So with new strategies, new innovations, and three million less crimes, you might think that clearance rates also showed a significant improvement in that same period of time—and you would be wrong. Have you ever taken a minute to think about the clearance rates for some of our most serious crimes in the United States? Would it surprise you to learn that the national clearance rate for robbery is 29.6 percent? If your home is burglarized today, there is a 13.6 percent chance that the offender will be arrested. During the same period discussed above when we saw a tremendous decrease in the number of crimes, violent crime clearance rates only improved 3 percent and property crime clearance rates only improved 2 percent. Not exactly the type of improvement one would expect. Many law enforcement agencies feel like they are fighting an uphill battle to make significant improvements to clearance rates.[40]

If you're murdered in America, there's a 1 in 3 chance that the police won't identify your killer. To use the FBI's terminology, the national "clearance rate" for homicide today is 64.1 percent. Fifty years ago, it was more than 90 percent. And that's worse than it sounds, because "clearance" doesn't equal conviction: It's just the term that police use to describe cases that end with an arrest, or in which a culprit is otherwise identified without the possibility of arrest—if the suspect has died, for example. Criminologists estimate that at least 200,000 murders have gone unsolved since the 1960s, leaving family and friends to wait and wonder.[41]

It is California's experience that puts the waiting period argument to rest. California has had a waiting period since 1923 and has regularly increased its length—from one day to three in 1955, to five days in 1965, and to 15 days in 1975. But as a study has revealed, while waiting periods were increasing so were murder rates, from two per 100,000 in 1952, to 10 by 1975. . . . The president, Congress, and state legislatures are constitutionally prevented from infringing on our right to bear arms, and a look at the statistics makes one question why they would want to anyway, since gun control hasn't worked where it has been tried. It is an authoritarian step in the wrong direction and a convenient distraction for people who don't want to deal with the real issues of removing from the streets the people who commit the crimes.[42]

CNS News reported the following: "The CDC's findings—that guns are an effective and often used crime deterrent and that most firearm incidents are not fatal—could affect the future of gun violence research." Here are some other highlights from the study:

"Self-defense can be an important crime deterrent," says a new report by the Centers for Disease Control (CDC). The $10 million study was commissioned by President Barack Obama as part of 23 executive orders he signed in January. "Studies that directly assessed the effect of actual defensive uses of guns (i.e., incidents in which a gun was 'used' by the crime victim in the sense of attacking or threatening an offender) have found consistently lower injury rates among gun-using *crime victims* compared with victims who used other self-protective strategies," the CDC study, entitled "Priorities For Research to Reduce the Threat of Firearm-Related Violence," states. The report, which notes that "violent crimes, including homicides specifically, have declined in the past five years," also pointed out that "some firearm violence results in death, but most does not." In fact, the CDC report said, most incidents involving the discharge of firearms do not result in a fatality. "In 2010, incidents in the U.S. involving firearms injured or killed more than 105,000 Americans, of which there were twice as many nonfatal firearm-related injuries (73,505) than deaths." . . . The Institute of Medicine and the National Research Council released the results of their research through the CDC last month. Researchers compiled data from previous studies in order to guide future research on gun violence, noting that "almost all national survey estimates indicate that *defensive* gun uses by victims are at least as common as *offensive* uses by criminals, with estimates of annual uses ranging from about 500,000 to more than 3 million per year." The article also stated that proposed "gun turn-in programs are ineffective."[43]

NOTES

1. NRA, quoted in Terry Hipp, *Last Call: Picking up the Sword of the Spirit* (Minneapolis, Minnesota: Mill City Press, 2012), 219.

2. Patrick Henry, quoted in Hugh A. Garland, *The Life of John Randolph of Roanoke*, vol. 1 (New York: D. Appleton and Company, 1856), 132.

3. Benjamin Franklin, proposition for the great seal of the United States.

4. Letter from Thomas Jefferson to Abigail Adams, February 22, 1787.

5. Fletcher Webster, ed., *The Writings and Speeches of Daniel Webster*, vol. 7 (1903), 47.

6. David B. Kopel, "Demonization of Guns," in *Guns in American Society: An Encyclopedia of History, Politics, Culture, and the Law*, ed. Gregg Lee Carter (Santa Barbara, California: ABC-CLIO, LLC, 2012).

7. Declaration of Independence; emphasis added.

8. Joseph Fielding Smith, in Conference Report, April 1950, 159.

9. Ezra Taft Benson, "A Witness and a Warning," *Ensign*, November 1979; emphasis added.

10. Declaration of Independence.

11. Letter from Thomas Jefferson to William Stephens Smith, November 13, 1787.

12. *The Writings of James Madison*, vol. 5, ed., Gaillard Hunt (New York: G. P. Putnam's Sons, 1904), 376–77.

13. Federalist Papers, no. 48.

14. Speech given at St. John's Church, Richmond, Virginia, March 23, 1775; famously known as the "Give Me Liberty or Give Me Death" speech.

15. US Constitution, Amend. II.

16. William M. Donnelly, "The Root Reforms and the National Guard," May 3, 2001, http://www.history.army.mil/documents/1901/Root-NG.htm; emphasis added.

17. US Constitution, Amend. 3.

18. Federalist Papers, no. 29.

19. Federalist Papers, no. 46.

20. Reply from Thomas Jefferson concerning Lord North's Proposition, 1775.

21. Letter from Thomas Jefferson to Samuel Adams, February 1800.

22. Letter from Thomas Jefferson to Thomas Cooper, September 10, 1814; see https://founders.archives.gov/documents/Jefferson/03-07-02-0471.

23. Thomas Jefferson, Sixth Annual Message, To the Senate and House of Representatives of the United States in Congress Assembled, December 2,

1806, http://www.lexrex.com/enlightened/writings/jefferson/sixthannual.htm.

24. "Mark Levin: We're Living in a Post-Constitutional America," *Real Clear Politics*, January 19, 2012, http://www.realclearpolitics.com/video/2012/01/19/mark_levin_were_living_in_a_post-constitutional_america.html.

25. See http://12160.info/profiles/blogs/surveillance-under-the-patriot-act-some-old-facts-but-all-so.

26. Thomas Jefferson, in the first draft of the Virginia Constitution, *The Papers of Thomas Jefferson*, 1776, https://www.monticello.org/site/jefferson/no-freeman-shall-be-debarred-use-arms-quotation.

27. Cesare Beccaria, "Essay on Crimes and Punishments," quoted in Thomas Jefferson, *Legal Commonplace Book*; see https://www.monticello.org/site/jefferson/laws-forbid-carrying-armsquotation#_ref-0.

28. Federalist Papers, no. 46.

29. James Madison, resolution for Amendments to the Constitution, no. 10, June 8, 1789, http://www.consource.org/document/madisons-resolution-for-amendments-to-the-constitution-1789-6-8/.

30. Patrick Henry, speech on the federal Constitution, Virginia Ratifying Convention, 1788.

31. *Federal Farmer*, no. 18, January 25, 1788.

32. Samuel Adams (February 6, 1788), in *Debates and Proceedings in the Convention of the Commonwealth of Massachusetts* (Boston: William White, 1850), 86.

33. George Washington, first annual State of the Union Address, January 8, 1790.

34. Letter from George Washington to George Mason, April 5, 1769.

35. "Declaration of Rights," no. 3, in the Convention of the State of North Carolina, on the Adoption of the Federal Constitution, July 21, 1788.

36. Federalist Papers, no. 28.

37. James Otis, "The Rights of the British Colonies Asserted and Proved (1764)," in *Classics of American Political and Constitutional Thought: Origins through the Civil War*, Scott J. Hammond, Kevin R. Hardwick, Howard L. Lubert, eds. (Indianapolis, Indiana: Hackett Publishing Company, 2007), 54.

38. George Mason, in Jonathan Elliot, *The Debates in the Several State Conventions on the Adoption of the Federal Constitution as Recommended by the General Convention at Philadelphia in 1787*, vol. 3 (New York: Burt Franklin, 1888), 380.

CHAPTER ELEVEN

39. Bowers vs. DeVito, 686 F.2d 616 (7th Cir., 1982); emphasis added.

40. Bob Scully (President of the National Association of Police Organizations, Washington, D.C.), in letter to the author, March 24, 1993.

41. Martin Kaste, "Open Cases: Why One-Third of Murders in America Go Unsolved," *NPR*, March 30, 2015, http://www.npr .org/2015/03/30/395069137/open-cases-why-one-third-of-murders-in -america-go-unresolved.

42. Pete du Pont, former governor of Delaware and chair of the Committee for American Leadership, in *Insight*, December 27, 1993.

43. Alissa Tabirian, "CDC Study: Use of Firearms For Self-Defense is 'Important Crime Deterrent,'" *CNSNews.com*, July 17, 2013; emphasis added.

TWELVE

The Usurpation of the Sovereign Powers of the State Governments

N o political dreamer was ever wild enough to think of breaking down the lines which separate the states, and of compounding the American people into one common mass."[1]

ALEXANDER HAMILTON

> The principles established in a former paper teach us that the States will retain all *pre-existing* authorities which may not be exclusively delegated to the federal head.[2]

> The plan of the convention declares that the power of Congress, or, in other words, of the *national legislature*, shall extend to certain enumerated cases. This specification of particulars evidently excludes all pretension to a general legislative authority, because an affirmative grant of special powers would be absurd.[3]

Originally, the states had complete jurisdiction over *domestic* concerns, such as health, education, welfare, business regulation, safety, and more. The people of each state and locality were able to choose their own level of government regulation and intervention in the lives of the citizens by the establishment of their own community standards. The Founding Fathers recognized the preexisting authority of the state governments, and created a national government with limited and restricted powers, a federal government with multiple levels for multiple purposes; with multiple checks on power, multiple balances on the use of power, and respect for the individual citizen from whom their power was derived.

Checks and balances were provided *within* the national government and *on* the national government. Everyone knows about the concept of the separation of powers: the legislative branch makes the laws, the executive branch enforces the laws, and the judicial branch adjudicates criminal accusations. However, additional checks and balances, *that were just as important*, were placed *on* the national government by the vertical separation of powers. These have been lost, for the most part, by changes made to our national government, but without amendments to the Constitution and rather by the expansive interpretation of a few clauses in the Constitution by the Supreme Court since the post-reconstruction period. The separation of powers between the state and the national governments are all but completely gone with the ratification of the Seventeenth Amendment. No longer is the revenue-raising ability of the national government restricted by citizens' purchase choices. No longer is the national government barred from the domestic concerns of the states, as provided by the Constitution and the Tenth Amendment. No longer is the federal government barred from affecting the lives of individual citizens directly. (Note: the average federal income tax paid by individual citizens in 1948 was only eight dollars. How much did you pay last year?)

THE FAR-REACHING POWER OF THE NATIONAL GOVERNMENT

Today, using the "General Welfare" and "Interstate Commerce" clauses, the Supreme Court allows the national government to do *anything* it wants to do, with little respect for the Constitution. Originally, however, the section that contained the "General Welfare" and "Interstate Commerce" clauses was meant to be a *limitation* on the power of the national government; limiting its power to tax and spend to those purposes listed in Section 1, and that were for the uniform welfare of *all* Americans; that is, for those purposes that all taxpayers would benefit from *equally*.

JAMES MADISON

Had no other enumeration or definition of the powers of the Congress been found in the Constitution, than the general expressions just cited [for the common defense and general welfare of the United States], the authors of the objection might have had some color for it. . . . But what color can the objection have, when a specification of the objects alluded to by these general terms immediately follows, and is not even separated by a longer pause than a semicolon? If the different parts of the same instrument ought to be so expounded, as to give meaning to every part which will bear it, shall one part of the same sentence be excluded altogether from a share in the meaning; and shall the more doubtful and indefinite terms be retained in their full extent, and the clear and precise expressions be denied any signification whatsoever? For what purpose could the enumeration of particular powers be inserted, if these and all others were meant to be included in the preceding general power? Nothing is more natural nor common than first to use a general phrase, and then to explain and qualify it by a recital of particulars.[4]

ARTICLE I, SECTION 8, OF THE CONSTITUTION

The Congress shall have Power To lay and collect taxes, duties, imposts and excises, to pay the debts and provide for the common defense and general welfare of the United States; but all duties, imposts and excises shall be uniform throughout the United States;

To borrow money on the credit of the United States;

To regulate commerce with foreign nations, and among the several states, and with the Indian tribes;

To establish an uniform rule of naturalization, and uniform laws on the subject of bankruptcies throughout the United States;

To coin money, regulate the value thereof, and of foreign coin, and fix the standard of weights and measures;

To provide for the punishment of counterfeiting the securities and current coin of the United States;

To establish post offices and post roads;

To promote the progress of science and useful arts, by securing for limited times to authors and inventors the exclusive right to their respective writings and discoveries;

To constitute tribunals inferior to the Supreme Court;

To define and punish piracies and felonies committed on the high seas, and offenses against the law of nations;

To declare war, grant letters of marque and reprisal, and make rules concerning captures on land and water;

To raise and support armies, but no appropriation of money to that use shall be for a longer term than two years;

To provide and maintain a navy;

To make rules for the government and regulation of the land and naval forces;

To provide for calling forth the militia to execute the laws of the union, suppress insurrections and repel invasions;

To provide for organizing, arming, and disciplining, the militia, and for governing such part of them as may be employed in the service of the United States, reserving to the States respectively, the appointment of the officers, and the authority of training the militia according to the discipline prescribed by Congress;

To exercise exclusive legislation in all cases whatsoever, over such District (not exceeding ten miles square), as may, by cession of particular states, and the acceptance of Congress, become the seat of the government of the United States, and to exercise like authority over all places purchased by the consent of the legislature of the state in which the same shall be for the erection of forts, magazines, arsenals, dockyards, and other needful buildings;—And

To make all laws which shall be necessary and proper *for carrying into execution the foregoing powers*, and all other powers vested by this Constitution in the government of the United States, or in any department or officer thereof.[5]

Just as James Madison said, the "specification of the objects alluded to by these general terms" to provide for the common defense and general welfare of the United States "immediately follows, and is not even separated by a longer pause than a semicolon."[6] It is clear that the intent of the Founding Fathers was to restrict governmental action to those powers specifically enumerated in the document itself. Any additional powers, that the people wanted given to government, would have to go through the amendment process defined in Article V of the Constitution:

> The *Congress*, whenever two thirds of both houses shall deem it necessary, shall propose amendments to this Constitution, *or, on the application of the legislatures of two thirds of the several states*, shall call a convention for proposing amendments, which, in either case, shall be valid to all intents and purposes, as part of this Constitution, when ratified by the legislatures of three fourths of the several states, or by conventions in three fourths thereof, as the one or the other mode of ratification may be proposed by the Congress; provided that no amendment which may be made prior to the year one thousand eight hundred and eight shall in any Manner affect the first and fourth clauses in the ninth section of the first article; and that no state, without its consent, shall be deprived of its equal suffrage in the Senate.[7]

Today, Senators and members of Congress who are wanting to expand the powers of the national government have been successful in getting the Supreme Court to allow the usurpation of powers from the states under the new, and expansive, definition of the "General Welfare" and "Interstate Commerce" clauses. This expansive definition of these clauses has allowed the national government to create one agency after another to regulate the American people. In effect, this has allowed Congress to create laws (agency regulations) for which they cannot be held responsible. They think that government needs to act for whatever reason, and they create a agency of experts to make regulations, which they put under the executive branch of government. When their constituents complain, they blame the executive branch agency they created! They can also assist the citizens with their problem with the agency while being viewed as a savior all the while.

The simple fact that so much of our government bureaucracy has been created without amendments to the Constitution proves that the Constitution is currently "hanging by a thread," and that we need to "awake to our awful situation." What is actually worse is that the American people have not only allowed this, but have often promoted it for their own selfish interests: social security, unemployment insurance, myriad entitlement programs, and so on.

ALEXANDER HAMILTON

> The welfare of the community [of state] is the only legitimate end for which money can be raised on the community. Congress can be considered as only under one restriction, which does not apply to other governments. They cannot rightfully apply the money they raise to any purpose merely or purely local. . . . The constitutional *test* of a right application must always be, whether it be for a purpose of *general* or *local* nature.[8]

JAMES MADISON

> If Congress can employ money indefinitely to the general welfare, and are the sole and supreme judges of the general welfare, they may take the care of religion into their own hands; . . . they may take into their own hands the education of children, establishing in like manner schools throughout the Union; . . . they may undertake the regulation of all roads other than post-roads; in short, every thing, from the highest object of state legislation down to the most minute object of police, would be thrown under the power of Congress; for every object I have mentioned would admit the application of money, and might be called, if Congress pleased, provisions for the general welfare.[9]

DAVY CROCKETT

> Mr. Speaker, I have as much . . . sympathy . . . as any man in this House; but . . . Congress has no power to appropriate this money as an act of charity. Every Member upon this floor knows it. We have the right, as individuals, to give away as much of our own money as we please in charity; but as Members of Congress we have no right so to appropriate a dollar of the public money.[10]

ANDREW JACKSON

> We are in no danger from violations of the Constitution from which encroachments are made upon the personal rights of the citizen. . . . But against the dangers of unconstitutional acts which, instead of menacing the vengeance of offended authority, proffer local advantages and bring in their train the patronage of government, we are, I fear, not so safe.[11]

GROVER CLEVELAND

> The lessons of paternalism ought to be unlearned and the better lesson taught that while the people should patriotically and cheerfully support their government, its functions do not include the support of the people.[12]

THOMAS JEFFERSON

> Congress had no unlimited powers to provide for the general welfare, but were restrained to those specifically enumerated.[13]

JAMES MADISON

> The government of the United States is a definite [a defined] government, confined to specified objects. It is not like the state governments, whose powers are more general. Charity is no part of the legislative duty of the government.[14]

> Mr. Madison . . . could not undertake to lay his finger on that article in the Federal Constitution which granted a right to

Congress of expending, on objects of benevolence, the money of their constituents.[15]

NOTES

1. Chief Justice Marshall, in McCulloch vs. Maryland, 1819.
2. Federalist Papers, no. 82; emphasis added.
3. Federalist Papers, no. 83; emphasis added.
4. Federalist Papers, no. 41.
5. US Constitution, Art. I, Sec. 8; emphasis added.
6. Federalist Papers, no 41.
7. US Constitution, Art. V; emphasis added.
8. Alexander Hamilton, "Hamilton's Argument on the Constitutionality of a Bank of the United States, February 1791," in Jonathan Elliot, *The Debates in the Several State Conventions on the Adoption of the Federal Constitution as Recommended by the General Convention at Philadelphia in 1787*, vol. 4 (New York: Burt Franklin, 1888), 618; emphasis in original.
9. James Madison, "On the Cod Fishery Bill, February 3, 1792," in *The Debates in the Several State Conventions, on the Adoption of the Federal Constitution, as Recommended by the General Convention at Philadelphia in 1787*, vol. 4 (Philadelphia: J. B. Lippincott and Co., 1863), 429.
10. Davy Crockett, in "David Crockett's Electioneering Tour," in *Harper's New Monthly Magazine*, vol. 34, December 1866 to May 1867 (New York: Harper and Brothers, Publishers, 1867), 607.
11. Andrew Jackson, quoted in Thomas James Norton, *The Constitution of the United States: Its Sources and Its Application* (Boston: Little, Brown, and Company, 1922), 45–46.
12. Glover Cleveland, second inaugural address, March 4, 1893.
13. Thomas Jefferson, quoted in *Abridgment of the Debates of Congress, from 1789 to 1856*, vol. 10 (New York: D. Appleton and Company, 1859), 473.
14. James Madison, speaking for the relief of St. Domingo refugees, January 10, 1794.
15. Speaking of James Madison, in Annals of Congress, House of Representatives, 3rd Congress, 1st Session, 170.

THIRTEEN

The Loss of a Constitution-Based Federal Judiciary

THOMAS JEFFERSON

> On every question of construction, carry ourselves back to the time when the Constitution was adopted, recollect the spirit manifested in the debates, and instead of trying what meaning may be squeezed out of the text, or invented against it, conform to the probable one in which it was passed.[1]

THE DANGER OF THE SUPREME COURT

ERNEST L. WILKINSON

> It may further interest you to know that on August 23, 1958, the chief justices of 36 state supreme courts, in a conference at Pasadena, California, in an unprecedented action, adopted a formal resolution, accusing the judges of the US Supreme Court of abusing their Constitutional powers. The Honorable M. T. Phelps, Senior Justice of the Arizona Supreme Court, said, "It is the design and purpose of the U.S. Supreme Court to usurp the policy-making powers of the nation. . . . By its own unconstitutional pronouncements, it would create an all-powerful, centralized government in Washington and subsequent destruction of

every vestige of States Rights expressly and clearly reserved to the States under the Tenth Amendment of the Constitution."

I honestly view the Supreme Court with its present membership and predilection, a greater danger to our democratic form of government and the American way of life than all forces aligned against us outside our boundaries.

Since that time the Supreme Court, in my judgment, has become even more arrogant in setting itself up as the god of our political life.[2]

Robert Bork made a very powerful point in his book *The Tempting of America*.[3] He argued that only when the Supreme Court restricts itself to interpreting laws in light of the original intent of the framers of the law in question—no matter how long ago or outdated by contemporary standards—can we maintain a "participatory democracy." If a Supreme Court ruling is not to the liking of the American people, then they can have it changed through the democratic branch of government—the legislature. Then, the next time a similar case is brought before the Supreme Court, they can rule on it using the contemporary intent of the legislature. This way the people get to establish their own standards through the legislature versus having an unelected, unaccountable group of nine men and women setting the standards for the nation. This way the written social contract of the people is honored and the people retain the power.

JAMES MADISON

The powers delegated by the proposed Constitution to the federal government are few and defined. Those which are to remain in the State governments are numerous and indefinite. The former will be exercised principally on external objects, as war, peace, negotiation, and foreign commerce; with which last the power of taxation will, for the most part, be connected. The powers reserved to the several States will extend to all the objects which, in the ordinary course of affairs, concern the lives, liberties, and properties of the people.[4]

ALEXANDER HAMILTON

The plan of the [constitutional] convention declares that the power of Congress . . . shall extend to certain enumerated cases. This specification of particulars evidently excludes all pretension to a general legislative authority, because an affirmative grant of special powers would be absurd, as well as useless, if a general authority was intended.[5]

JAMES MADISON

The operations of the federal government will be most extensive and important in times of war and danger; those of the State governments, in times of peace and security.[6]

THE SUPREME COURT'S ABANDONMENT OF THE CONSTITUTION

So what happened to the original intent and understanding of this clause?

With Franklin D. Roosevelt (FDR), the federal government abandoned our Constitution: FDR proposed "New Deal" schemes; Congress passed them. At first, the Supreme Court opined (generally 5 to 4) that "New Deal" programs were unconstitutional as outside the powers granted to Congress. But when FDR threatened to "pack the court" by adding judges who would do his bidding, one judge flipped to the liberal side, and the Court started approving New Deal programs (generally 5 to 4).

Since then, law schools don't teach the Constitution. Instead, they teach Supreme Court opinions which purport to explain why Congress has the power to regulate anything it pleases. The law schools thus produced generations of constitutionally illiterate lawyers and judges who have been wrongly taught that the "general welfare" clause, along with the "interstate commerce" and the "necessary and proper" clauses, permit Congress to do whatever it wants![7]

Using a very contemporary example, Roger Pilon of the Cato Institute succinctly *identified the problem*, "*Is it unconstitutional for Congress to mandate that individuals buy health insurance or be taxed if they don't? Absolutely—if we lived under the Constitution. But we don't.* Today we live under something called 'constitutional law'—an accumulation of 220 years of Supreme Court opinions—and that 'law' reflects the Constitution only occasionally."[8]

ALEXANDER HAMILTON

It can be of no weight to say that the courts, on the pretense of a repugnancy, may substitute their own pleasure to the constitutional intentions of the legislature. This might as well happen in the case of two contradictory statutes; or it might as well happen in every adjudication upon any single statute. The courts must declare the sense of the law; and if they should be disposed to exercise WILL instead of JUDGMENT, the consequence would equally be the substitution of their pleasure to that of the legislative body. . . . To avoid an arbitrary discretion in the courts, it is indispensable that they should be bound down by strict rules and precedents, which serve to define and point out their duty in every particular case that comes before them. . . .

There is no position which depends on clearer principles, than that every act of a delegated authority, contrary to the tenor of the commission under which it is exercised, is void. No legislative act, therefore, contrary to the Constitution, can be valid. To deny this, would be to affirm, that the deputy is greater than his principal; that the servant is above his master; that the representatives of the people are superior to the people themselves; that men acting by virtue of powers, may do not only what their powers do not authorize, but what they forbid. . . . It is not otherwise to be supposed, that the Constitution could intend to enable the representatives of the people to substitute their WILL to that of their constituents. It is far more rational to suppose, that the courts were designed to be an intermediate body between the people and the legislature, in order, among other things, to keep the latter within the limits assigned to their authority. . . . Nor does this conclusion by any means suppose a superiority of the judicial to the legislative power. It only supposes that the power of the people is superior to both; and that where the will of the legislature, declared in its statutes, stands in opposition to that of the people, declared in the Constitution, the judges ought to be governed by the latter rather than the former. They ought to regulate their decisions by the fundamental laws, rather than by those which are not fundamental.[9]

Today we have a Supreme Court with a history of judicial activism, (judicial legislation or judicial administration), which is completely in opposition to the spirit and the letter of the law as found in the Constitution. One knowledgable student of history has explained it this way:

This is often done under the aegis of necessity because the federal courts complain there are social needs which are not being met by the states or the Congress. . . . It has been employed repeatedly by the Supreme Court on the ground that the judiciary is merely carrying out "established public policy." This is a dangerous crutch to sustain judicial activism, since slavery was once "established public policy." Policies are set by Congress, not the courts. The court's arena relates to "laws" and "rights," not policies.

The increase in judicial activism has been creeping upward for years [based upon this reasoning] . . . [and] it began reversing previous Supreme Court decisions. . . . It also became heavily involved in administrative duties, including the administration of state school systems, state prisons, and state employment policies.

Even earlier, the court unlawfully laid the foundation for what turned out to be an amendment to the Constitution in the 1936 Butler case, where *general welfare* was twisted to allow *special* welfare, and the federal budget jumped from six billion [dollars] to six *hundred* billion [dollars] in one generation.

The Warren court then went on to wipe out the right of the states to deal with subversion and internal security. . . . It reduced to virtual extinction the states' residence requirements for voters, made the states elect their state senators on the basis of population instead of senatorial districts, imposed federal standards of procedure on local police, sustained executive orders imposing federal standards of air, water, speed, safety, and health on the states, and otherwise made serious invasions into the sovereign and exclusive domain of the states. . . . Much of the judicial activism was with good intentions and high moral aspirations. But the delivery system was wrong, the administrative system was wrong, and the results were corrosive and corruptive to the constitutional system.[10]

It is clear from the writings of the Founders that this was not supposed to be. Hamilton, in the Federalist Papers, argued that the court could take "no active resolution whatever," and that it was the "weakest of the three departments of power."[11] It is interesting that some of the Founders realized the one omission to the Constitution was that there was no *real* check on the power of the judicial branch.

THOMAS JEFFERSON

It has long however been my opinion . . . that the germ of dissolution of our federal government is in the constitution of the federal judiciary . . . working like gravity by night and by day, gaining a little to-day and a little tomorrow, and advancing it's noiseless step like a thief, over the field of jurisdiction, until all shall be usurped from the states, and the government of all be consolidated into one. To this I am opposed; because, whenever all government . . . shall be drawn to Washington as the center of all power, it will render powerless the checks provided . . . and will become as venal and oppressive as the government from which we separated.[12]

There were two safety nets provided though in the Constitution: (1) Article V, which gives the states the power to call a constitutional convention (which has yet to ever happen), and (2) the "Right of the Jury," which was removed by the Supreme Court in 1895. With the "right of the jury" intact, the members of the jury, if they felt a particular law was unjust or unconstitutional, could bring in a verdict of "not guilty" no matter what the Congress or the courts said. As we discussed earlier, this is another check and balance that has been lost.

THOMAS JEFFERSON

There is no danger I apprehend so much as the consolidation of our government by the noiseless, and therefore unalarming, instrumentality of the supreme court.[13]

GEORGE WASHINGTON

But let there be no change by usurpation; for though this, in one instance, may be the instrument of good, it is the customary weapon by which free governments are destroyed. The precedent must always greatly overbalance in permanent evil any partial or transient benefit which the use can at any time yield.[14]

JAMES MADISON

Because it is proper to take alarm at the first experiment on our liberties. We hold this prudent jealousy to be the *first* duty of citizens, and one of the *noblest* characteristics of the late Revolution. The free men of America did not wait till usurped power had strengthened itself by exercise, and entangled the question in precedents. *They saw all the consequences in the principle, and they avoided the consequences by denying the principle.*[15]

THE VIRGINIA RATIFICATION OF THE CONSTITUTION OF THE UNITED STATES

We the Delegates of the people of Virginia, duly elected in pursuance of a recommendation from the General Assembly, and now met in Convention, having fully and freely investigated and discussed the proceedings of the Federal Convention, and being prepared as well as the most mature deliberation hath enabled us, to decide thereon, Do, in the name and in behalf of the people of Virginia, *declare and make known, that the powers granted under the Constitution, being derived from the people of the United States may be resumed by them whensoever the same shall be perverted to their injury or oppression, and that every power not granted thereby remains with them and at their will: that therefore no right of any denomination, can be cancelled, abridged, restrained or modified, by the Congress, by the Senate or House of Representatives acting in any capacity, by the President or any department or officer of the United States, except in those instances in which power is given by the Constitution for those purposes: and that among other essential rights, the liberty of conscience and of the press cannot be cancelled, abridged, restrained or modified by any authority of the United States.* . . . We the said Delegates, in the name and in behalf of the people of Virginia, do by these presents assent to, and ratify the Constitution recommended on the seventeenth day of September, one thousand seven hundred and eighty seven, by the Federal Convention for the Government of the United States.[16]

NOTES

1. Paul Leicester Ford, comp., *The Writings of Thomas Jefferson*, vol. 10, 1816–1826 (New York: Knickerbocker Press, 1899), 231.

2. "The Changing Nature of American Government from a Constitutional Republic to a Welfare State," Ernest L. Wilkinson, *FreeRepublic*, January 25, 2017, www.freerepublic.com/focus/f-chat/1792784/posts.

3. Robert H. Bork, *The Tempting of America: The Political Seduction of the Law* (Free Press, 1997).

4. Federalist Papers, no. 45.

5. Federalist Papers, no. 83.

6. Federalist Papers, no. 45.

7. "Does the 'General Welfare Clause' of the U.S. Constitution Authorize Congress to Force Us to Buy Health Insurance?," Publius Huldah,

Publius-Huldah's Blog, January 25, 2017, publiushuldah.wordpress.com/category/general-welfare-clause/.

8. Roger Pilon, "Healthcare: Is 'mandatory insurance' unconstitutional?," *The Arena*, September 18, 2009, www.politico.com/arena/perm/Roger_Pilon_972633D2-0728-48D6-9626-9A2149A6C0EF.html; emphasis added.

9. Federalist Papers, no. 78.

10. W. Cleon Skousen, *The Making of America: The Substance and Meaning of the Constitution* (Washington, D.C.: National Center for Constitutional Studies, 1985), 255–56; emphasis in original.

11. Federalist Papers, no. 78.

12. Letter from Thomas Jefferson to C. Hammond, August 18, 1821.

13. Thomas Jefferson, quoted in Hamilton A. Long, *Your American Yardstick* (Your Heritage Books, 1963), 41.

14. George Washington, Farewell Address, September 19, 1796.

15. US Constitution, Amend. 1; emphasis added.

16. "Virginia's Ratification," *U.S. Constitution Online*, February 2, 2017, www.usconstitution.net/rat_va.html; emphasis added.

FOURTEEN
The Loss of a Balanced Budget and Fiscal Responsibility

THOMAS JEFFERSON

> The question whether one generation has the right to bind another by the deficit it imposes is a question of such consequence as to place it among the fundamental principles of government. We should consider ourselves unauthorized to saddle posterity with our debts and morally bound to pay them ourselves.[1]

GEORGE WASHINGTON

> No pecuniary consideration is more urgent than the regular redemption and discharge of the public debt; on none can delay be more injurious, or an economy of time more valuable.[2]

BENJAMIN FRANKLIN

> But ah! think what you do when you run in debt; you give to another power over your liberty.[3]

JOHN ADAMS

> The consequences arising from the continual accumulation of public debts in other countries ought to admonish us to be careful to prevent their growth in our own. The national defense must

be provided for as well as the support of Government; but both should be accomplished as much as possible by immediate taxes, and as little as possible by loans.[4]

KEITH HALL, DIRECTOR OF THE CONGRESSIONAL BUDGET OFFICE

The long-term outlook for the federal budget has worsened dramatically over the past several years.[5]

THOMAS JEFFERSON

I wish it were possible to obtain a single amendment to our Constitution; I would be willing to depend on that alone for the reduction of the administration of our government to the genuine principles of its Constitution; I mean an additional article taking from the federal government the power of borrowing.[6]

It is a wise rule and should be fundamental in a government disposed to cherish its credit, and at the same time to restrain the use of it within the limits of its faculties, "never to borrow a dollar without laying a tax in the same instant for paying the interest annually, and the principal within a given term."[7]

A 1987 study of congressional expenditures for the previous forty years (and it has not gotten better since) has shown that Congress has spent $1.58 for every $1.00 it has raised in new taxes. During the years of President Bush (1988–1992), that number grew to $1.83 for every $1.00 raised in new taxes. The question: "Is the present attempt by the executive and legislative branches of the federal government to sell the American people on higher taxes really the answer?" They have already proven, over the last fifty years, that higher taxes *only* means higher spending. They have never addressed the national debt—or even the yearly deficit. The only way to return our government to fiscal responsibility is to absolutely refuse higher taxes, and demand spending cuts.

The United States was spending $9.397 billion per day in 2015 with a $532 billion deficit. This is $10,712 per year for every man, woman, and child in America. The deficit for 2015 was $1,662 for every man, woman, and child in the country using 320.09 million as the population. In 2013, there were 138.3 million taxpayers; so, spending was approximately $24,801 per taxpayer.[8]

Where is all this money going? Most of it, you will see below, goes to entitlement programs that our politicians use to purchase votes to get reelected. It is not all their fault, however, since we elected them and continue to reelect them. According to the Pulitzer Prize-winning Politifact website, "Congress ha[d] 11% approval ratings but 96% incumbent reelection rate" after the 2014 elections.[9]

I would bring your attention to a few scriptures in Doctrine and Covenants 124:

> 1 We believe that governments were instituted of God for the benefit of man; *and that he holds men accountable for their acts in relation to them*, both in making laws and administering them, for the good and safety of society. . . .
> 3 We believe that all governments necessarily require civil officers and magistrates to enforce the laws of the same; and that such as will administer the law in equity and justice should be sought for and upheld *by the voice of the people if a republic*, or the will of the sovereign. (D&C 124:1, 3; emphasis added)

Since we live in a democratic, constitutional republic, we are responsible to our Heavenly Father for who we vote for, the political principles we hold, how well informed we are regarding the Constitution (which He endorsed), and how we uphold its principles. We read in Doctrine and Covenants 98:

> 4 And now, verily I say unto you concerning the laws of the land, it is my will that my people should observe to do all things whatsoever I command them.
> 5 And that law of the land which is constitutional, supporting that principle of freedom in maintaining rights and privileges, belongs to all mankind, and is justifiable before me.

6 Therefore, I, the Lord, justify you . . . in befriending [supporting] that law which is the constitutional law of the land;

7 And as pertaining to law of man, whatsoever is more or less than this, cometh of evil. (D&C 98:4–7)

And in Doctrine and Covenants 101 we read:

76 And again I say unto you . . . it is my will that they should continue to importune for redress, and redemption, by the hands of those who are placed as rulers and are in authority over you—

77 According to *the laws and constitution of the people, which I have suffered to be established, and should be maintained for the rights and protection of all flesh*, according to just and holy principles;

78 *That every man may act in doctrine and principle pertaining to futurity, according to the moral agency which I have given unto him, that every man may be accountable for his own sins in the day of judgment.*

79 Therefore, it is not right that any man should be in bondage one to another.

80 And for this purpose have I established the Constitution of this land, by the hands of wise men whom I raised up unto this very purpose, and redeemed the land by the shedding of blood. (D&C 101:76–80; emphasis added)

It is clear that there is a price for the liberty we have been given under the Constitution; it is a requirement to have an understanding and knowledge of it, as it was given to us by our Fathers as inspired by the Father, so that we can recognize any political proposal which is "more or less than this" (D&C 98:7). We have this moral responsibility to safeguard the liberty we have been given for future generations, and be able to recognize the moment when the Elders of Israel need to step forward to save it! Think about it: the greatest evil you can do to others is to empower government to restrict their life, liberty, or property. Short of becoming another Hitler, Stalin, or Mao Tse-tung, there is nothing that you can possibly do during your life than to participate in enacting or supporting ill conceived laws that will tax or regulate your neighbors, or make criminals of them through the enacted law.

The Heritage Foundation report referenced above concluded, "Debt is too high, and growing"; "In 2014, the national debt exceeds $145,000 per American household"; "Net interest cost will double in five years, nearly triple in eight"; "Obamacare's new spending will cost more than $1.8 trillion over the next decade for its massive expansion of Medicaid and subsidies for those purchasing health insurance in the new exchanges"; and "Food stamps are one of the largest and fastest-growing means-tested welfare programs [where] . . . costs have doubled in inflation-adjusted terms since 2008 [with] . . . more than 46 million Americans receiv[ing] food stamps every month."[10] To put all our government spending into perspective, the Heritage Foundation uses this analogy: "In 2014, a median-income family will earn about $52,000. If a typical family followed the federal government's lead, it would spend nearly $60,400 and put $8,400 on a credit card. This family would have already racked up more than $308,800 in credit card debt—like a mortgage, only without the house."[11] In case this doesn't register, they went on to list fifty-one examples of government waste and mismanagement.

According to a report from the Government Accountability Office, duplication of federal programs and services could cost taxpayers $45 billion annually.[12]

During the first one hundred years of the United States, Congress tried to control the spending and pay of the national debt whenever they could. As I am writing this on March 22, 2016, the US Debt Clock shows the US national debt to be over $19 *trillion* and growing. This not only includes the "official" numbers given to us by the president, but also the sum of all entitlement programs to which we have committed ourselves.

We are all aware of the wasteful spending programs our national government is involved in, but look at the costs of some programs you may not have questioned before. According to NationalPriorities.org, "*Every hour*, federal taxpayers in the United States pay $2.93 million towards Foreign Aid, $6.74 million for Homeland Security [which includes immigration and customs who have their hands tied by our current president], and $40.68 million for Medicaid and the Children's Health Insurance Program in 2016."[13]

The information for the chart below comes from the US Government Publishing Office, and can be found on their website: www.gpo.gov. Look at the significant increases in spending by nearly *all* agencies.

OUTLAYS BY AGENCY: 2000 AND 2015 COMPARED (IN MILLIONS OF DOLLARS)[14]

Department or Unit	2000	2015	% Increase
Legislative Branch	2,871	4,694	163%
Judicial Branch	4,057	7,584	187%
Dept. of Agriculture	75,071	139,727	186%
Dept. of Commerce	7,788	9,607	123%
Dept. of Defense	281,028	584,319	208%
Dept. of Education	33,476	76,334	228%
Dept. of Energy	14,971	29,374	196%
Dept. of Health and Human Services	382,311	1,010,384	264%
Dept. of Homeland Security	13,159	47,456	361%
Dept. of Housing and Urban Development	30,781	38,088	124%
Dept. of the Interior	7,998	13,702	171%
Dept. of Justice	16,846	33,859	201%
Dept. of Labor	31,873	68,094	214%
Dept. of State	6,687	28,954	433%
Dept. of Transportation	41,555	84,252	203%
Dept. of the Treasury	390,524	572,593	147%
Dept. of Veterans Affairs	47,044	158,039	336%
Corps of Engineers—Civil Works	4,229	7,745	183%
Other Defense Civil Programs	32,801	57,368	175%
Environmental Protection Agency	7,223	8,379	116%

Department or Unit	2000	2015	% Increase
Executive Office of the President	283	506	179%
General Services Administration	74	488	659%
International Assistance Programs	12,087	21,577	179%
National Aeronautics and Space Administration	13,428	18,076	135%
National Science Foundation	3,448	8,103	235%
Office of Personnel Management	48,655	93,362	192%
Small Business Administration	-421	1,057	-251%
Social Security Admin. (On-Budget)	45,121	90,398	200%
Social Security Admin. (Off-Budget)	396,169	870,808	220%

The problem is not *just* the amount of money the national government is collecting, or *how* it is collecting it through *graduated* income taxes for the most part, but also the fact that our government is *shackling our posterity* to pay for programs for which we receive the "benefits" through deficit spending. Doing an analysis of the *Summary of Receipts, Outlays, and Surpluses or Deficits: 1789–2021* from the Office of Management and Budget,[15] this is how budget deficits have been trending:

Period	Years of Deficit Spending	Percent of Years with Deficits
1901–1930	9	30%
1931–1960	23	77%
1961–2001	36	88%
2002–2015	14	100%

Now, it is not just a matter of the size of these deficits—usually in the hundreds of billions per year—but it is also a matter of the amount we are spending each year to service the accumulated debt. This table from the US Treasury Department shows how the *interest* payment per year has virtually doubled since 1988:[16]

Fiscal Year End	Interest Expense	Fiscal Year End	Interest Expense
2016	$432,649,652,901.12	2001	$359,507,635,242.41
2015	$402,435,356,075.49	2000	$361,997,734,302.36
2014	$430,812,121,372.05	1999	$353,511,471,722.87
2013	$415,688,781,248.40	1998	$363,823,722,920.26
2012	$359,796,008,919.49	1997	$355,795,834,214.66
2011	$454,393,280,417.03	1996	$343,955,076,695.15
2010	$413,954,825,362.17	1995	$332,413,555,030.62
2009	$383,071,060,815.42	1994	$296,277,764,246.26
2008	$451,154,049,950.63	1993	$292,502,219,484.25
2007	$429,977,998,108.20	1992	$292,361,073,070.74
2006	$405,872,109,315.83	1991	$286,021,921,181.04
2005	$352,350,252,507.90	1990	$264,852,544,615.90
2004	$321,566,323,971.29	1989	$240,863,231,535.71
2003	$318,148,529,151.51	1988	$214,145,028,847.73
2002	$332,536,958,599.42		

Come on! Isn't it time to listen to your own common sense instead of the "experts"? Tell the truth—doesn't this scare you just a little? How long could your family operate with major deficits every year? If this does scare you, then welcome to the real world, a world that *our* complacency created by allowing our representatives to use these financial practices.

SPENDING, DEBT, AND ACCOUNTABILITY

We will be held responsible for our decisions, including who we voted to represent us. And don't you think those men and women who voluntarily gave up their lives, liberty, or property for their posterity will ask us what we did to be frugal while protecting our rights? We have a duty to be "eternally vigilant" and not to trust just any person with the reins of government. Let us consider this scripture:

> 34 Behold, there are many called, but few are chosen. And why are they not chosen?

35 Because their hearts are set so much upon the things of this world, and aspire to the honors of men, that they do not learn this one lesson—

36 That the rights of the priesthood are inseparably connected with the powers of heaven, and that the powers of heaven cannot be controlled nor handled [except] upon the principles of righteousness . . .

37 They may be conferred upon us, it is true; but when we undertake to cover our sins, or to gratify our pride . . . or to exercise control or dominion or compulsion upon the souls of the children of men . . . behold, the heavens withdraw themselves; the Spirit of the Lord is grieved; and when it is withdrawn, Amen to the priesthood or the authority of that man.

39 We have learned by sad experience that it is the nature and disposition of almost all men, as soon as they get a little authority, as they suppose, they will immediately begin to exercise unrighteous dominion.

40 Hence many are called, but few are chosen. (D&C 121:34–37, 39–40)

One way we "exercise control or dominion or compulsion upon the souls of the children of men" (D&C 121:37) is through the way we vote in our constitutional republic, the political platforms we support, and the men and women we vote for during elections for political office. We will be held accountable; how can it be otherwise when we have been given so much? How can it be otherwise when we are shackling future generations with our debts? Let's stop apologizing for free enterprise and American political principles (limited government, self-reliance, hard work, individual liberty, the right to own and control property, the difficulty in constitutionally amending the Constitution), and demand a resurgence of these principles by our representatives and in our educational institutions.

MILTON FRIEDMAN, NOBEL-PRIZE-WINNING ECONOMIST

> For the period from the founding of this country to 1929, leaving aside periods of major wars such as the Civil War and the First World War and the Revolution, total government spending in the United States (federal, state, and local), never exceeded 10 percent of the income of the people. State and local expenditure more immediately subject to the control of the citizenry was twice as large during that period as federal government expenditures. Total federal government expenditure in 1929 was 3 percent of the national income. In the forty-five years since, total governmental expenditures have risen to 40 percent of the national income in the United States and federal government spending is twice as much as state and local spending. Federal spending today is something like 25 percent of the national income, or roughly 10 times as large as it was in 1929. We have been moving in the same direction as Chile and Britain and New York [which declared bankruptcy], and we have been experiencing signs of financial crisis—the emergence of inflation at a higher and higher rate. We have also been experiencing the second effect: the loss of freedom.[17]

Financially, this is our situation: about two-thirds of the spending by the national government is unconstitutional. As you read through this list of national agencies; you will either find justification for them plainly in the text of Article I, Section 8, or you will find that they are unconstitutional regardless of what the Supreme Court has ruled, and therefore the spending is not authorized for their purposes.

OUTLAYS BY AGENCY: 1962–2016 (IN MILLION DOLLARS)[18]

Department or Unit	2015	% of Total	Constitutional Spending	Unconstitutional Spending
Legislative Branch	4,694	0.12%	0.12%	
Judicial Branch	7,548	0.19%	0.19%	

Department or Unit	2015	% of Total	Constitutional Spending	Unconstitutional Spending
Dept. of Agriculture	139,727	3.58%		3.58%
Dept. of Commerce/US Census	9,607	0.25%	0.25%	
Dept. of Defense	584,319	14.98%	14.98%	
Dept. of Education	76,334	1.96%		1.96%
Dept. of Energy	29,374	0.75%		0.75%
Dept. of Health and Human Services	1,010,384	25.90%		25.90%
Dept. of Homeland Security: ICE, TSA, Citizenship and Immigration Service, Border Patrol, Customs Service	47,456	1.22%	1.22%	The TSA is unconstitutional and an assault on our rights.
Dept. of Housing and Urban Development	38,088	0.98%		0.98%
Dept. of the Interior	13,702	0.35%		0.35%
Dept. of Justice	33,859	0.87%	0.87%	
Dept. of Labor	68,094	1.75%		1.75%
Dept. of State	28,954	0.74%	0.74%	
Dept. of Transportation	84,252	2.16%		2.16%

Department or Unit	2015	% of Total	Constitutional Spending	Unconstitutional Spending
Dept. of the Treasury	572,593	14.68%	14.68%	
Dept. of Veterans Affairs	158,039	4.05%	4.05%	
Corps of Engineers— Civil Works	7,745	0.20%		0.20%
Other Civil Defense Programs	57,368	1.47%	1.47%	
Environmental Protection Agency	8,379	0.21%		0.21%
Executive Office of the President	506	0.01%	0.01%	
General Services Administration	488	0.01%	0.01%	
International Assistance Programs	21,577	0.55%		0.55%
National Aeronautics and Space Administration	18,076	0.46%	0.46%	
National Science Foundation	8,103	0.21%		0.21%
Office of Personnel Management	93,362	2.39%	2.39%	
Small Business Administration	1,057	0.03%		0.03%

Department or Unit	2015	% of Total	Constitutional Spending	Unconstitutional Spending
Social Security Administration (On-Budget)	90,398	2.32%		2.32%
Social Security Administration (Off-Budget)	870,808	22.32%		22.32%
Other Independent Agencies (On-Budget)	19,413	0.50%		0.50%
Total outlays	3,900,989		41.45%	63.76%

You may think that some of the agencies I have listed are worth having, and I am sure I will agree with you on a few of them, but if the American people thought they were absolutely necessary functions of the national government, a constitutional amendment would have easily passed. Some agencies, such as NASA, should be moved back under the Department of Defense to be constitutional; others like the FBI, should be a clearinghouse for the exchange of data between the states only and have very limited enforcement capabilities.

An unpleasant truth that most try to avoid is that the only true security that we can find in this world is through Jesus Christ, and He tests us to prove our worthiness and chastens us when we stand in need of correction. The place where most people look for security is the government, which is an institution of force, and therefore, is based upon the principles of Satan. Whenever we look to government to provide us security from the consequences of our actions, we thwart the purpose of our existence: to learn and become more like our Savior. Why should people look any farther than a government that promises cradle-to-grave security? What makes it even worse is that no government has ever been able to provide the security it promises for very long.

Here are some clear statements of American political principles in the words of the Founders:

THOMAS JEFFERSON

We shall all consider ourselves unauthorized to saddle posterity with our debts, and morally bound to pay them ourselves, and consequently within what may be deemed the period of a generation, or the life of the majority.[19]

The principle of spending money to be paid by posterity, under the name of funding, is but swindling futurity on a large scale.[20]

We are ruined, Sir, if we do not overrule the principles that "the more we owe, the more prosperous we shall be," "that a public debt furnishes the means of enterprise," "that if ours should be once paid off, we should incur another by any means however extravagant" etc. etc.[21]

I . . . place economy among the first and most important of republican virtues, and public debt as the greatest of the dangers to be feared.[22]

The public money of this country is the toil and labor of the people . . . reasonable frugality ought to be observed. And we would recommend particularly, the strictest care and the utmost firmness to prevent all unconstitutional draughts upon the public treasury.[23]

JAMES MADISON

A public debt is a public curse and, in a republican government, a greater one than in any other.[24]

GEORGE WASHINGTON

As a very important source of strength and security, cherish public credit . . . use it as sparingly as possible . . . avoiding likewise the accumulation of debt . . . in time of peace . . . discharge the debts, which unavoidable wars may have occasioned, not ungenerously throwing upon posterity the burthen [*sic*], which we ourselves ought to bear.[25]

CHAPTER FOURTEEN

ALEXANDER HAMILTON

> Ardently wishes to see it incorporated as a fundamental maxim in the system of public credit of the United States, that the creation of debt should always be accompanied with the means of extinguishment.[26]

> It is a general maxim, that all governments find a use for as much money as they can raise. Indeed, they have commonly demands for more. Hence it is that all, as far as we are acquainted, are in debt. I take this to be a settled truth, that they will all spend as much as their revenue; that is, will live at least up to their income. Congress will ever exercise their powers to levy as much money as the people can pay. They will not be restrained from direct taxes by the consideration that necessity does not require them.[27]

JOHN DICKINSON

> Honor, justice, and humanity call upon us to hold and to transmit to our posterity that liberty which we received from our ancestors. *It is not our duty to leave wealth to our children, but it is our duty, to leave liberty to them.* No infamy, iniquity, or cruelty can exceed our own, if we, born and educated in a country of freedom, entitled to its blessings and knowing their value, pusillanimously [cowardly] deserting the post assigned us be Divine Providence, surrender succeeding generations to a condition of wretchedness from which no human efforts, in all probability, will be sufficient to extricate them.[28]

Here is the danger in allowing the national government to utilize a direct tax and deficit spending:

THOMAS JEFFERSON

> With money we will get men, said Caesar, and with men we will get money. Nor should our assembly [the Virginia Legislature] be deluded by the integrity of their own purposes, and conclude that

these unlimited powers will never be abused, because themselves are not disposed to abuse them. They should look forward to a time, and that not a distant one, when a corruption in this, as in the country from which we derive our origin, will have seized the heads of government, and be spread by them through the body of the people; when they will purchase the voices of the people, and make them pay the price. Human nature is the same on every side of the Atlantic. . . . The time to guard against corruption and tyranny, is before they shall have gotten hold on us.[29]

JAMES MADISON

Some, who have not denied the necessity of the power of taxation, have grounded a very fierce attack against the Constitution, on the language in which it is defined. It has been urged and echoed, that the power "to lay and collect taxes, duties, imposts, and excises, to pay the debts, and provide for the common defense and general welfare of the United States," amounts to an unlimited commission to exercise every power which may be alleged to be necessary for the common defense or general welfare. No stronger proof could be given of the distress under which these writers labor for objections, than their stooping to such a misconstruction.[30]

NOTES

1. *Congressional Record*, vol. 156, pt. 2 (Washington, D.C.: United States Government Printing Office, 2010), 5057.
2. Jared Sparks, *The Life of George Washington* (London: Henry Colburn, 1839), 265.
3. Benjamin Franklin, *Memoirs of Benjamin Franklin* (Philadelphia: McCarty and Davis, 1884), 2:479.
4. John Adams, State of the Union Address, November 1797.
5. US Congressional Budget Office, "The 2015 Long-Term Budget Outlook" (June 2015), 1.
6. Letter from Thomas Jefferson to John Taylor, November 1798.
7. Letter from Thomas Jefferson to John Wayles Eppes, June 24, 1813.

8. Scott Greenburg, "Summary of the Latest Federal Income Tax Data, 2015 Update," *Tax Foundations*, November 19, 2015, https://taxfoundation.org /summary-latest-federal-income-tax-data-2015-update.

9. Louis Jacobson, "Congress Has 11% Approval Ratings But 96% Incumbent Reelection Rate, Meme Says," *Politifact*, November 11, 2014, http://www .politifact.com/truth-o-meter/statements/2014/nov/11/facebook-posts /congress.

10. Romina Boccia, "Federal Spending by the numbers, 2014: Government Spending Trends in Graphics, Tables, and Key Points (Including 51 Examples of Government Waste)," *Heritage Foundation*, December 8, 2104, http://www.heritage.org/research/reports/2014/12 /federal-spending-by-the-numbers-2014.

11. Ibid.

12. Ibid.

13. "Cost of National Security," *National Priorities Project*, last modified May 28, 2015, https://www.nationalpriorities.org/cost-of/; emphasis added.

14. "Historical Tables, Budget of the United States Government, Fiscal Year 2015," March 10, 2014, https://www.gpo.gov/fdsys/granule /BUDGET-2015-TAB/BUDGET-2015-TAB-4-1.

15. Office of Management and Budget, "Summary of Receipts, Outlays, and Surpluses or Deficits: 1789–2021," https://obamawhitehouse.archives.gov /omb/budget/Historicals.

16. "Interest Expense on the Debt Outstanding," *TreasuryDirect*, last modified January 5, 2017, https://www.treasurydirect.gov/govt/reports/ir/ir_expense .htm.

17. Milton Friedman, "The Fragility of Freedom," *BYU Studies* 16, no. 4 (Summer 1976), https://byustudies.byu.edu/content/fragility-freedom.

18. See https://www.gpo.gov/fdsys/granule/BUDGET-2015-TAB/BUDGET -2015-TAB-4-1.

19. Letter from Thomas Jefferson to John Wayles Eppes, September 1813.

20. Letter from Thomas Jefferson to John Taylor, May 1816.

21. Letter from Thomas Jefferson to James Monroe, April 1791.

22. Letter from Thomas Jefferson to William Plumer, July 1816.

23. Letter from Town of Braintree, Massachusetts, to Rep. Ebenezer Thayer, in *The Political Writings of John Adams*, ed. George A. Peek Jr. (Indianapolis, Indiana: Hackett Publishing Company, 1954), 25.

24. James Madison, quoted in Lance Banning, *The Sacred Fire of Liberty: James Madison and the Founding of the Federal Republic* (Ithaca: Cornell University Press, 1995), 315.

25. George Washington, Farewell Address, September 19, 1796.

26. Alexander Hamilton, "Report on Manufactures: House of Representatives, May 23," in *Register of Debates in Congress, Comprising the Leading Debates and Incidents of the First Session of the Twenty-Second Congress*, vol. 8 (Washington, D.C.: Gales and Seaton, 1833), 80.

27. In Jonathan Elliot, *The Debates in the Several State Conventions on the Adoption of the Federal Constitution as Recommended by the General Convention at Philadelphia in 1787*, vol. 2 (New York: Burt Franklin, 1888), 333.

28. John Dickinson, quoted in William C. Armor, *Lives of the Governors of Pennsylvania with the Incidental History of the State* (Philadelphia: James K. Simon, 1872), 240; emphasis added.

29. Thomas Jefferson, *Notes on the State of Virginia* (Boston: Lilly and Wait, 1832), 124–25.

30. Federalist Papers, no. 41.

FIFTEEN

The Establishment of an "Imperial Congress"

O ur Founding Fathers were moral and virtuous men—regardless of what you have been taught during the last fifty years of public education in this country. They were altruistic in their motives and dedicated to providing their posterity with liberty. The Lord's declaration that He raised the Founding Fathers up to perform the work of providing liberty to this country, and their visit to Wilford Woodruff in the St. George Temple should be enough proof of this statement.

WILFORD WOODRUFF

> I will here say, before closing, that two weeks before I left St. George, the spirits of the dead gathered around me, wanting to know why we did not redeem them. Said they, "You have had the use of the Endowment House for a number of years, and yet nothing has ever been done for us. We laid the foundation of the government you now enjoy, and we never apostatized from it, but we remained true to it and were faithful to God." These were the signers of the Declaration of Independence, and they waited on me for two days and two nights. I thought it very singular, that notwithstanding so much work had been done, and yet nothing had been done for them. The thought never entered my heart, from the

191

fact, I suppose, that heretofore our minds were reaching after our more immediate friends and relatives. I straightway went into the baptismal font and called upon Brother McCallister to baptize me for the signers of the Declaration of Independence, and fifty other eminent men, making one hundred in all, including John Wesley, Columbus, and others; I then baptized him for every President of the United States, except three; and when their cause is just, somebody will do the work for them.[1]

The Founders were not men seeking power or gain from their efforts to free their fellow citizens from the shackles of a monarch, or from their efforts to provide us with a constitutional government that would last until we destroyed it from within, as we are doing when we support "income distribution" programs, or are willing to give up liberty for security from every fear. There was no campaigning during the early years of the United States. A man was promoted for a position by others who had known his character and seen his work ethic. They were not going around the country making promises to voters, and saying, "Vote for me!" This was beneath them, and should be beneath our leaders today as well. What started as citizens selecting tried and proven leaders, has turned into a circus of empty promises, name calling, and negative campaigning.

THE ORIGINAL CONGRESS VS. TODAY'S CONGRESS

Under the initial Constitution, senators and members of Congress were to meet "at least once in every year, and such meeting shall be on the first Monday in December."[2] Having them meet in December, the last month of the year, should give us some idea of how long the Founders envisioned the Congress should be in session. They met after the harvests were in and they could afford to leave their real pursuits. They held down real jobs and lived with their families in the districts that they represented. They had to return to their hometowns and face their neighbors and fellow citizens, to be accountable directly for their voting record. They didn't have large congressional staffs to write letters justifying their positions on all political issues: they had to do it face-to-face with the people they lived among for eleven out of the twelve months of each year. They also were private citizens without special privileges, and they had to live by the laws they passed for the rest of society.

According to the US Department of Commerce's report *Income and Poverty in the United States: 2014*, issued in September 2014, there were 46.7 million Americans living in poverty. The median household income in 2014 was $53,657.[3] Now let us compare this to the income of members of the House of Representatives and the Senate: "The most recent pay adjustment for Members of Congress was in January 2009. Since then, the compensation for most Senators, Representatives, [and so on] has been $174,000. The only exceptions include the Speaker of the House ($223,500) and the President pro tempore of the Senate and the majority and minority leaders in the House and Senate ($193,400)."[4]

> "Various options are available to Members regarding participation in the Civil Service Retirement System (CSRS) and the Federal Employees Retirement System (FERS). . . . [It] varies depending on retirement plan, age, and length of service. . . . Since January 1, 1984, participation in Social Security has been mandatory for all Members of Congress." In addition to their salary, they also receive a Member Representational Allowance (MRA) for "Supporting Personnel, Office Expenses, Travel to the District, and Mail for Members of the House," which is used for personnel to help them get reelected and maintain their office, worth "$944,671 for each Member in 2016." In addition to this, they receive "official office expenses, which varies among Members due to variations in the distance between a Member's district and Washington, D.C., and the cost of General Services Administration office rental space in the district; official (franked) mail, which varies among Members based on the number of nonbusiness addresses in the district. . . . The three components are combined. . . . In 2016, . . . the MRAs range[d] from $1,207,510 to $1,383,709, with an average

of $1,268,520." "Each Member may use the MRA to employ no more than 18 permanent employees" to help them maintain their position in office. If you are a Senator, you get even more money. "The Senators' Official Personnel and Office Expense Account (SOPOEA)" ranges from "$3,043,454 to $4,815,203. The average allowance is $3,306,570." Now look at how well other employees of Congress are paid: "Speaker of the House: $223,500 per annum; Majority and Minority Leaders: $193,400 per annum; Inspector General: $172,500 per annum." And now for the officers of the Senate: President pro tempore and Majority and Minority Leaders: $193,400 per annum.[5]

All of these imperial salaries are three times more than the average American makes. And Congress is causing the problems for which we have to pay.

The following excerpt comes from an article, entitled "Government Policies Caused the Financial Crisis and Made the Recession Worse":

Start with [the government's] completely arbitrary goal of increasing home ownership when most qualified homebuyers already own homes. Add to the mix government-sanctioned . . . lower credit standards along with abundant financing. . . . One doesn't need a Ph.D. in economics to predict this combination of policies will lead to higher consumer debt, higher home prices, and an unstable financial system.[6]

Add this to unjustified, offensive wars which destroy American lives, the devaluing of the dollar which affects us all, billions of dollars in wasteful spending, and the destruction of the constitutional rights guaranteed in the Bill of Rights by the "Patriot" Act, and you might wonder why we pay the government officials anything at all. So, while Senators and members of Congress are living very well, on our money, they are causing major problems for the American people, which they then blame on others, while we are left to pay for their mistakes. What a great job. No wonder they are willing to spend millions of dollars campaigning for their positions.

CHAPTER FIFTEEN

IS CONGRESS ABOVE THE LAW?

Another example of an imperial Congress who exempts themselves from the laws they pass can be found in the article "How Congress Puts Itself Above the Law." A portion of the article is included here:

> For years, some have argued that we need a Twenty-Eighth Amendment to the Constitution providing that all members of Congress have to comply with all laws that other citizens have to obey. "Congress shall make no law," the amendment might read, "that applies to the citizens of the United States that does not apply equally to the senators and/or representatives; and, Congress shall make no law that applies to the senators and/or representatives that does not apply equally to the citizens of the United States."
> . . . Over the decades, Congress has passed innumerable statutes that regulate every aspect of life in the American workplace, then quickly exempted themselves. In 1938, when the Fair Labor Standards Act established the minimum wage, the 40-hour workweek, and time and a half for overtime, Congress exempted. . . . In 1964, with great fanfare, President Johnson signed the landmark Civil Rights Act, including Title VII, which for the first time protected all Americans from employment discrimination on the basis of race, color, religion, sex or national origin. But the law exempted Congress from its coverage. . . . The same blanket congressional exemption found in Title VII was contained in a total of 10 other federal statutes regulating the American workplace. . . .
> America shouldn't need to amend the Constitution to ensure that elected leaders comply with the laws of the land. But given the sorry history of congressional leadership by exemption rather than by example, a Twenty-Eighth Amendment doing precisely that makes sense.[7]

At one time or another, Congress has exempted itself from the Americans with Disabilities Act, two Civil Rights Acts, the Freedom of Information Act, the Age Discrimination Act, the Occupational

Safety and Health Act, and the Ethics in Government Act. If these are not imperial acts, I do not know what are.

JAMES MADISON

> I will add, as a fifth circumstance in the situation of the House of Representatives, restraining them from oppressive measures, that they can make no law which will not have its full operation on themselves and their friends, as well as on the great mass of the society. This has always been deemed one of the strongest bonds by which human policy can connect the rulers and the people together. It creates between them that communion of interests and sympathy of sentiments, of which few governments have furnished examples; but without which every government degenerates into tyranny. If it be asked, what is to restrain the House of Representatives from making legal discriminations in favor of themselves and a particular class of the society? I answer: the genius of the whole system; the nature of just and constitutional laws; and above all, the vigilant and manly spirit which actuates the people of America, a spirit which nourishes freedom, and in return is nourished by it. If this spirit shall ever be so far debased as to tolerate a law not obligatory on the legislature, as well as on the people, the people will be prepared to tolerate any thing but liberty.[8]

> It is a sound and important principle that the representative ought to be acquainted with the interests and circumstances of his constituents [by themselves having to work for a living outside of their government positions].[9]

BENJAMIN FRANKLIN

> Sir, there are two passions which have a powerful influence in the affairs of men. These are *ambition* and *avarice*; the love of power and the love of money. Separately, each of these has great force in prompting men to action; but when united in view of the same object, they have in many minds the most violent effects. Place before the eyes of such men a post of *honor* that shall at the same

time be a place of *profit*, and they will move heaven and earth to obtain it. . . . And of what kind are the men that will strive for this profitable preeminence . . . ? It will not be the wise and moderate, the lovers of peace and good order, the men fittest for the trust. It will be the bold and the violent, the men of strong passions and indefatigable activity in their selfish pursuits. These will thrust themselves into your government, and be your rulers. And these, too, will be mistaken in the expected happiness of their situation; for their vanquished competitors of the same spirit and from the same motives, will perpetually be endeavoring to distress their administration, thwart their measures, and render them odious to the people.[10]

MR. NICHOLAS

We have the best security we can wish for: if they impose taxes on the people which are oppressive, they subject themselves . . . to the same inconvenience.[11]

JAMES MADISON

The Accumulation of all powers, legislative, executive, and judiciary, in the same hands, whether of one, a few, or many, and whether hereditary, self-appointed, or *elective*, may justly be pronounced the very definition of tyranny.[12]

It will be of little avail to the people, that the laws are made by men of their own choice, if the laws be so voluminous that they cannot be read, or so incoherent that they cannot be understood; if they . . . undergo such incessant changes that no man, who knows what the law is to-day, can guess what it will be to-morrow. Law is defined to be a rule of action; but how can that be a rule, which is little known, and less fixed? . . . Every new regulation concerning commerce or revenue, or in any manner affecting the value of the different species of property, presents a new harvest to those who watch the change, and can trace its consequences; a harvest, reared not by themselves, but by the toils and cares of the great body of their fellow-citizens.[13]

Is there no virtue among us? If there be not, we are in a wretched situation. No theoretical checks—no form of government can render us secure. To suppose that any form of government will secure liberty of happiness without any virtue in the people, is a chimerical [comical] idea.[14]

ABRAHAM LINCOLN

If our American society and United States Government are overthrown, it will come from the voracious desire for office, the wriggle to live without toil, work, and labor—from which I am not free myself.[15]

THE COST OF THE BUREAUCRACY

Along with the "imperial" Congress, we are also paying for an "imperial" bureaucracy.

The federal government employs 2.1 million civilian workers in hundreds of agencies at offices across the nation. The federal workforce imposes a substantial burden on America's taxpayers. In 2016 wages and benefits for executive branch civilian workers cost $267 billion. Since the 1990s, federal workers have enjoyed faster compensation growth than private-sector workers. In 2015 federal workers earned 76 percent more, on average, than private-sector workers. Federal workers earned 42 percent more, on average, than state and local government workers. The federal government has become an elite island of secure and high-paid employment, separated from the ocean of average Americans competing in the economy.[16]

NOTES

1. Wilford Woodruff, in *Journal of Discourses*, 19:229.
2. US Constitution, Art. I, Sec. 4.

3. Carmen DeNavas-Walt, Bernadette D. Proctor, "Income and Poverty in the United States: 2014," *United States Census Bureau*, September 2015, http:// www.census.gov/library/publications/2015/demo/p60-252.html.

4. "Salaries of Members of Congress: Recent Actions and Historical Tables," 4, in *Congressional Research Service Reports*, https://digital.library.unt.edu /ark:/67531/metadc806486/m1/4/?q=97-1011.

5. "Congressional Salaries and Allowances: In Brief, December 30, 2014– July 14, 2016," *EveryCRSReport.com*, https://www.everycrsreport.com /reports/RL30064.html; accessed on February 4, 2017.

6. Norbert J. Michel, "Government Policies Caused the Financial Crisis and Made the Recession Worse," *Forbes*, January 26, 2015, http://www.forbes .com/sites/norbertmichel/2015/01/26/government-policies-caused-the -financial-crisis-and-made-the-recession-worse/#3995b24661bf.

7. Gerald D. Skoning, "How Congress Puts Itself Above the Law," *The Wall Street Journal*, April 15, 2013, https://www.wsj.com/articles/SB1000142412 7887324504704578413182814140480.

8. Federalist Papers, no. 57.

9. Federalist Papers, no. 56.

10. Benjamin Franklin, "Speech of Dr. Franklin in the Convention on the Subject of Salaries," in *Memoirs of the Life and Writings of Benjamin Franklin*, ed. William Temple Franklin, vol. 1 (Philadelphia: T. S. Manning, 1818), 469.

11. Mr. Nicholas, in Jonathan Elliot, *The Debates in the Several State Conventions on the Adoption of the Federal Constitution as Recommended by the General Convention at Philadelphia in 1787*, vol. 3 (New York: Burt Franklin, 1888), 99.

12. Federalist Papers, no. 47; emphasis added.

13. Federalist Papers, no. 62.

14. James Madison, speech in the Virginia Ratifying Convention, June 20, 1788.

15. Abraham Lincoln, quoted in *The Politics and Law of Term Limits*, ed. Edward H. Crane Roger Pilon (Washington, D.C.: Cato Institute, 1994), 35.

16. Chris Edwards, "Reducing the Costs of Federal Worker Pay and Benefits," *Downsizing the Federal Government*, September 20, 2016, accessed February 4, 2017, http://www.downsizinggovernment.org /federal-worker-pay.

SIXTEEN

Unauthorized Criminal Laws and the National Government

nder the Constitution and written within its text, the national government has the power to define and enforce punishment for criminal acts in only certain areas: (1) "Piracies and felonies committed on the high seas," (2) "counterfeiting the securities and current coin of the United States," (3) "treason," and to (4) "exercise exclusive legislation in all cases whatsoever over [the] District [of Columbia]."[1] Other than crimes committed on the high seas or within the District of Columbia, the national government has no policing powers of any sort concerning crimes; these were left to the states to define and enforce. This was a critical part of the vertical separation of powers between the state and national governments. It left to the level of government that was closest to the people the power to define and enforce laws relating to crime; ultimately, the final say was left to the jury (we the people) concerning punishments for crimes committed. If a jury of peers could not be convinced of the criminality of a person's action, then the law had no force in that specific case.

In addition to this, the Fifth Amendment to the Constitution, as part of the Bill of Rights, guarantees that "No person shall be held to answer for a capital, or otherwise infamous crime, unless on a presentment or indictment of a Grand Jury. . . . nor shall any person be subject for the same offence to be twice put in jeopardy of life or limb; nor shall be compelled in any criminal case to be a witness against himself, nor be deprived of life, liberty, or property, without due process of law."[2] This is referred to as the "Double Jeopardy" clause, and it prohibits the national government from prosecuting individual citizens for the same crime more than once, or imposing more than one punishment for a single crime. Each of our fifty states has similar protections for citizens in their constitutions. This constitutional provision was considered "a universal Maxim of the common law" and dated back to the Romans and Greeks.[3]

Here is a good legal discussion on where double jeopardy applies:

> Only certain types of legal proceedings invoke double jeopardy protection. If a particular proceeding does not place an individual in jeopardy, then subsequent proceedings against the same individual for the same conduct are not prohibited. The Fifth Amendment suggests that the protection against double jeopardy extends only to proceedings that threaten "life or limb." Nevertheless, the US Supreme Court has established that the right against double jeopardy is not limited to capital crimes or Corporal Punishment, but that it extends to all felonies, misdemeanors, and juvenile-delinquency adjudications, regardless of the applicable punishments.
>
> In Benton vs. Maryland, 395 US 784, 89 S. Ct. 2056, 23 L. Ed. 2d 707 (1969), the US Supreme Court ruled that the federal Double Jeopardy Clause is applicable to state and federal prosecutions. Prior to this ruling, an individual who was accused of violating state law could rely only on that particular state's protection against double jeopardy. Some states offered greater protection than others did. The Court, relying on the doctrine of incorporation, which makes fundamental principles in the Bill of Rights applicable to the states through the EQUAL PROTECTION CLAUSE of the Fourteenth Amendment, said this was not permissible. The right against double jeopardy is so important, the Court concluded, that it must be equally conferred upon the citizens of

every state. Under *Benton*, no state may provide its residents with less protection against double jeopardy than that offered by the federal Constitution.

The US Supreme Court has also held that the right against double jeopardy precludes only subsequent *criminal* proceedings. It does not preclude ordinary civil or administrative proceedings against a person who already has been prosecuted for the same act or omission. Nor is prosecution barred by double jeopardy if it is preceded by a final civil or administrative determination on the same issue.

Courts have drawn the distinction between criminal proceedings on the one hand, and civil or administrative proceedings on the other, based on the different purposes served by each. Criminal proceedings are punitive in nature and serve two primary purposes: deterrence and retribution. Civil proceedings are more remedial; their fundamental purpose is to compensate injured persons for any losses incurred. Because civil and criminal remedies fulfill different objectives, a government may provide both for the same offense.

The multiple legal proceedings brought against O. J. (Orenthal James) Simpson in the death[s] of Nicole Brown Simpson and Ronald Lyle Goldman illustrate these various objectives. The state of California prosecuted Simpson for the murders of his former wife and her friend. Despite Simpson's acquittal in the criminal case, three civil suits were filed against him by the families of the two victims. The criminal proceedings were instituted with the purpose of punishing Simpson, incarcerating him, and deterring others from similar behavior. The civil suits were intended to make the victims' families whole by compensating them with money damages for the losses they had suffered.[4]

What we learn from this is that double jeopardy only applies in multiple criminal cases for the same offense but does not bar citizens harmed by the actions of another from suing in civil court for compensation of their losses. What happens when *both* the state and national governments have laws defining criminal actions? Let's look at hate crimes as examples. The FBI says of them:

> Hate crimes are the highest priority of the FBI's Civil Rights program, not only because of the devastating impact they have on families and communities, but also because groups that preach hatred and intolerance can plant the seed of terrorism here in our country. . . . A hate crime is a traditional offense like murder, arson, or vandalism with an added element of bias. For the purposes of collecting statistics, the FBI has defined a hate crime as a "criminal offense against a person or property motivated in whole or in part by an offender's bias against a race, religion, disability, sexual orientation, ethnicity, gender, or gender identity." Hate itself is not a crime—and the FBI is mindful of protecting freedom of speech and other civil liberties.[5]

So, now we have double jeopardy where an "offense like murder, arson, or vandalism" may be prosecuted at the state level, but where the national government can file a claim against the acquitted person for a hate crime because the federal prosecutor believes the offender was "in part" motivated by their "bias against" the victim's "race, religion, disability, sexual orientation, ethnicity, gender, or gender identity." This sounds like double jeopardy to me. Now let's look at how prolific the national government has been in coming up with new crimes.

According to an article in the *Wall Street Journal*,

> The U.S. Constitution mentions three federal crimes by citizens: treason, piracy and counterfeiting. By the turn of the 20th century, the number of criminal statutes numbered in the dozens. Today, there are an estimated 4,500 crimes in federal statutes, according to a 2008 study by retired Louisiana State University law professor John Baker.

There are also thousands of regulations that carry criminal penalties. Some laws are so complex, scholars debate whether they represent one offense, or scores of offenses.

Counting them is impossible. The Justice Department spent two years trying in the 1980s, but produced only an estimate: 3,000 federal criminal offenses.

The American Bar Association tried in the late 1990s, but concluded only that the number was likely much higher than 3,000. The ABA's report said "the amount of individual citizen behavior now potentially subject to federal criminal control has increased in astonishing proportions in the last few decades."

A Justice spokeswoman said there was no quantifiable number. Criminal statutes are sprinkled throughout some 27,000 pages of the federal code. . . . Those expressing concerns include the American Civil Liberties Union and Edwin Meese III, former attorney general under President Ronald Reagan. Mr. Meese, now with the conservative Heritage Foundation, argues Americans are increasingly vulnerable to being "convicted for doing something they never suspected was illegal."

"Most people think criminal law is for bad people," says Timothy Lynch of Cato Institute, a libertarian think tank. People don't realize "they're one misstep away from the nightmare of a federal indictment."[6]

Federal crime means those acts that are made criminal or illegal by federal law and prosecuted in federal courts. For instance, kidnapping is a federal crime. Most federal crimes are listed in Title 18 of the United States Code, but some fall under other titles. For example, tax evasion is made a federal crime under Title 26 of the United States Code. It is also called as federal offense. The power to investigate federal crime is granted to the Federal Bureau of Investigation (FBI).[7]

CRIME ON A GOVERNMENT LEVEL

We also need to remember these words of Lysander Spooner: "The greatest of all *crimes* are the wars that are carried on by governments, to plunder, enslave, and destroy mankind."[8] Government is *the* greatest threat to our liberty and peace. When we allow the government to create new laws, we do so at our own peril. What I believe we are seeing in this country today is the breakdown of the respect each citizen feels toward its government because of the ridiculous nature of the laws it is creating, while at the same time it is refusing to enforce some basic laws, such as immigration and border security.

LOUIS C. BRANDEIS

Crime is contagious. If the Government becomes a lawbreaker, it breeds contempt for law.[9]

Spooner continues to define crime based upon its severity:

The next greatest crimes committed in the world are equally prompted by avarice and ambition; and are committed, not on sudden passion, but by men of calculation, who keep their heads cool and clear, and who have no thought whatever of going to prison for them.

They are committed, not so much by men who *violate* the laws, as by men who, either by themselves or by their instruments, *make* the laws—by men who have combined to usurp arbitrary power, and to maintain it by force and fraud, and whose purpose in usurping and maintaining it is by unjust and unequal legislation, to secure to themselves such advantages and monopolies as will enable them to control and extort the labor and properties of other men, and thus impoverish them, in order to minister to their own wealth and aggrandizement. The robberies and wrongs thus committed by these men, *in conformity with the laws,*—that is, *their own laws*—are as mountains to molehills, compared with the crimes committed by all other criminals, in *violation* of the laws.

But, thirdly, there are vast numbers of frauds of various kinds committed in the transactions of trade, whose perpetrators, by their coolness and sagacity, evade the operation of the laws. And it is only their cool and clear heads that enable them to do it. . . . Fourthly, the professed burglars, robbers, thieves, forgers, counterfeiters, and swindlers who prey upon society.[10]

How interesting is it that our greatest threats are from those we elect? The Lord has warned us of this:

28 And again, I say unto you that the enemy in the secret chambers seeketh your lives.
29 Ye hear of wars in far countries, and you say that there will soon be great wars in far countries, but ye know not the hearts of men in your own land. (D&C 38:28–29)

In this same section, He also tells us "Wherefore, hear my voice and follow me, and you shall be a free people, and *ye shall have no laws but my laws* when I come, for I am your lawgiver, and what can stay my hand?" (D&C 38:22; emphasis added). What are His laws? The Prophet Joseph Smith specified section 42 of the Doctrine and Covenants as "embracing the law of the Church" (D&C 42, section introduction):

18 And now, behold, I speak unto the church. Thou shalt not kill; and he that kills shall not have forgiveness in this world, nor in the world to come.
19 And again, I say, thou shalt not kill; but he that killeth shall die.
20 Thou shalt not steal; and he that stealeth and will not repent shall be cast out.
21 Thou shalt not lie; he that lieth and will not repent shall be cast out.
22 Thou shalt love thy wife with all thy heart, and shalt cleave unto her and none else.

23 And he that looketh upon a woman to lust after her shall deny the faith, and shall not have the Spirit; and if he repents not he shall be cast out.
24 Thou shalt not commit adultery; and he that committeth adultery, and repenteth not, shall be cast out.
25 But he that has committed adultery and repents with all his heart, and forsaketh it, and doeth it no more, thou shalt forgive;
26 But if he doeth it again, he shall not be forgiven, but shall be cast out.
27 Thou shalt not speak evil of thy neighbor, nor do him any harm.
28 Thou knowest my laws concerning these things are given in my scriptures; he that sinneth and repenteth not shall be cast out.
29 If thou lovest me thou shalt serve me and keep all my commandments. (D&C 42:18–29)

His laws are not complicated; complete bookshelves are *not* needed to explain them; they are simple and straightforward. They are summed up in these words:

24 And let every man esteem his brother as himself, and practice virtue and holiness before me.
25 And again I say unto you, let every man esteem his brother as himself. (D&C 38:24–25)

This is why we only learn of judges being selected by Moses and King Mosiah; there was no need for a legislature.

NOTES

1. US Constitution, Art. I, Sec. 6 and 8.
2. US Constitution, Amend. 5.
3. United States vs. Wilson, 420 US 340, (4th Cir. 1975).
4. "Double Jeopardy," *The Free Dictionary*, accessed February 4, 2017, http://legal-dictionary.thefreedictionary.com/double+jeopardy).
5. "What We Investigate: Hate Crimes," *FBI*, accessed February 4, 2017, https://www.fbi.gov/investigate/civil-rights/hate-crimes.

6. Gary Fields and John R. Emshwiller, "As Criminal Laws Proliferate, More Are Ensnared," *The Wall Street Journal*, July 23, 2011.

7. "Federal Crimes Law and Legal Definition," *USLegal*, accessed February 4, 2017, definitions.uslegal.com/f/federal-crimes%20/.

8. Dio Lewis, *Prohibition a Failure: Or, the True Solution of the Temperance Question* (Boston: James R. Osgood and Company, 1875), 133; emphasis added.

9. "Olmstead vs. United States: The Constitutional Challenges of Prohibition Enforcement," *Federal Judicial Center*, accessed February 4, 2017, www.fjc .gov/history/home.nsf/page/tu_olmstead_doc_15.html.

10. "Vices Are Not Crimes," Lysander Spooner and Murray N. Rothbard, *MisesInstitute*, mises.org/library/vices-are-not-crimes; emphasis in original.

SEVENTEEN

The Loss of Christianity as the Foundation of Government

The first ten amendments to the Constitution, called the Bill of Rights, were required by many of the state legislatures as a prerequisite to ratification of the Constitution. It is important to realize that the Bill of Rights was originally intended to be *a restriction on the national government only* and did *not* apply to the state governments, although most states had similar guarantees in their individual constitutions. The Founders considered the usurpation and intervention by the national government, in the affairs of the states and the people, to be the most serious threat to the happiness and welfare of the American society. Therefore, the Bill of Rights starts with a bold prohibition against national intervention in specific areas, by stating, *"Congress shall make no law . . ."*

It is also worth considering that the Founders did not want to have the national government serve as the watchdog over the states' responsibility to protect the rights of the people. Madison's proposed provision in the Bill of Rights that said, "No state shall violate the equal rights of conscience, or the freedom of the press, or the trial by jury in criminal cases," was quickly dismissed by the first Congress.[1]

A result of the application of the Bill of Rights to the state governments has been the total removal of anything religious in our educational and political systems *by the Supreme Court, which started just after World War II.* This was a total reversal from the position held by the Founding Fathers considering that seven of the thirteen original colonies had a *state church* founded on the Christian *religion*: (1) Connecticut, Congregational; (2) New Hampshire, Protestant; (3) Delaware, Christian; (4) New Jersey, Protestant; (5) Maryland, Christian; (6) South Carolina, Protestant; (7) Massachusetts, Congregational Church.[2]

THE REMOVAL OF RELIGION
AND LEGAL PRECEDENCE

The total removal of any mention or teaching of Christ has now been removed from the public educational system of the country, and from mention in our political discourse *by the Supreme Court* just since 1947. To understand how this has happened, we need to understand the concept of *stare decisis* or legal precedence.

In 2007, James H. Fowler of the University of California at San Diego, and Sangick Jeon of Stanford University researched this issue in *The Authority of Supreme Court Precedent*, and explained how "precedent" has become such an important issue to the Supreme Court, even contrary to the belief of the Founding Fathers, as expressed by President Andrew Jackson: "I cannot assent. Mere precedent is a dangerous source of authority, and should not be regarded as deciding questions of constitutional power."[3] Fowler and Jeon demonstrate "the evolution of the norm of *stare decisis* [precedence] in the 19th Century and a significant deviation from this norm by the activist Warren Court [1953–1969]."[4]

> Institutionally, the United States judiciary is the weakest of the three branches of government. In the words of Alexander Hamilton, the US Supreme Court was founded in the idea that they would have "no influence over either the sword or the purse, no direction either of the strength or of the wealth of the society . . . to have neither Force nor Will, but merely judgment; and must ultimately depend upon the aid of the executive arm for the efficacy of its judgments"

CHAPTER SEVENTEEN

(Madison et al., 1966 [1788]). . . . As a result, the Court suffered a crisis in institutional and decisional legitimacy, virtually powerless without the ability to enforce and implement their substantive decisions. Refusing nomination to the Court as chief justice, former Chief Justice John Jay wrote to President Adams in 1800, "I left the bench perfectly convinced that under a system so defective [the Court] would not . . . acquire the public confidence and respect which, as the last resort of justice in the nation, it should possess" (Baker, 1974, 332).

Legal historians suggest that justices in the 19th Century responded to the crisis of legitimacy by strengthening the norm of *stare decisis*, a legal norm inherited from English common law that encourages judges to follow precedent by letting the past decision stand (Friedman, 1985, 127–33). In order to foster compliance and enhance the institutional reputation of the Court, *stare decisis* was implemented to place decision-making in the domain of neutral legal principles and the "accumulated experience of many judges responding to the arguments and evidence of many lawyers" (Landes and Posner, 1976, 250) rather than at the whim of the personal preferences of individuals. To this day, the justices of the Supreme Court are aware of the inherent weakness of the federal judiciary and place high value on maintaining their institutional and decisional legitimacy through the use of precedent (Ginsburg, 2004; Powell, 1990; Stevens, 1983). Recognizing that legitimacy is essential to achieve their policy objectives, the members of the Court justify their substantive rulings through court opinions, which allow the justices to demonstrate how their decisions are consistent with existing legal rules and principles established in prior cases (see Hansford and Spriggs, 2006, 24–30). Because it is the application of existing precedents that creates the perception of judicial decision-making to be procedurally neutral and fair (Tyler and Mitchell, 1994), these opinions are often considered to be the source of the Court's power (Epstein and Knight, 1998; Segal and Spaeth, 2002).

Unfortunately, the exact role of law in Supreme Court decision-making is still quite unclear. Due to the complexity of law
and the difficulty in quantifying the concept of precedent, the
"[judicial] literature continues to present an underdeveloped theoretical and empirical understanding of why and when law changes"
(Hansford and Spriggs, 2006, 6). This problem has often pushed
judicial specialists to rely on the ideology of decisions and judges
rather than the content of court opinions and the role of law itself
to analyze judicial decision-making (George and Epstein, 1992).
This is unfortunate not only because of the vital function of court
opinions, but also because the literature has ignored a rich source
of accessible information about the role of precedent—the assessments of the justices themselves. Each *judicial citation* contained
in an opinion is essentially a latent judgment about the case cited.
When justices write opinions, they spend time researching the law
and selecting precedents to support their arguments. Thus, the
citation behavior of the Courts provides information about which
precedents serve important roles in the development of American
law.[5]

So, instead of determining the original intent of the legislature
which enacted the law, Supreme Court judges have developed this
system of precedence which enables them to cull through earlier decisions to "[select] precedents to support their arguments" or the precon-
ceived notions and biases. How is this supporting the Constitution,
and the democratic process? How is this safeguarding the rights of the
citizens they are sworn to protect? How is this doing much of anything other than usurping authority to make them feel better about
"suffer[ing] a crisis in institutional and decisional legitimacy, [and feeling] virtually powerless without the ability to enforce and implement
their . . . decisions," as Fowler and Jeon put it.[6]

What happens when the justices are so intoxicated by their assumed
power that they *create* the law, as they did in Roe vs. Wade? Robert H.
Bork's assessment of their decision was that,

The Court has used its invented privacy right exclusively to enforce sexual freedoms. The most dramatic instance was the success of the pro-abortion movement in evading democratic processes to lodge its desires in the Constitution, effectively making abortion a convenient birth control technique. The majority opinion in Roe v. Wade is a curious performance: In just over fifty-one pages it contains no shred of legal reasoning (or logic of any description), but simply announces that the right of privacy is sufficiently capacious [spacious] to encompass a woman's right to an abortion. The opinion laid down new rules more permissive than any state legislature had produced.[7]

Archibald Cox, former US solicitor general agreed, saying

The Justices read into the generalities of the Due Process Clause of the Fourteenth Amendment a new "fundamental right" not remotely suggested by the words. . . . The failure to confront the issue in principled terms leaves the opinion to read like a set of hospital rules and regulations. . . . Neither historian, layman, nor lawyer will be persuaded that all the details prescribed in Roe v. Wade are part of either natural law or the Constitution.[8]

Alexander Bickel, professor at Yale Law School, concluded:

One is left to ask why [the Court decided as it did in Roe vs. Wade]. The Court never said. It refused the discipline to which its function is properly subject. It simply asserted the result it reached. This is all the Court could do because moral philosophy, logic, reason, or other materials of law can give no answer. . . . It is astonishing that only two dissented from the Court's decision. . . . The dissenters were Justices Byron White and William Rehnquist. The Court's decision was an "extravagant exercise" of judicial power, said Justice White; it was a legislative rather than a judicial action, suggested Justice Rehnquist. So it was, and if the Court's guess on the probable and desirable direction of progress is wrong, that guess will nevertheless have been imposed on all fifty states.[9]

ANDREW JACKSON

> I cannot assent. Mere precedent is a dangerous source of authority, and should not be regarded as deciding questions of constitutional power.[10]

THOMAS JEFFERSON

> One single object . . . [will merit] the endless gratitude of the society: that of restraining the judges from usurping legislation.[11]

Today the Supreme Court bases its decisions on precedence over the original intent of the legislature; and primarily on court decisions made after World War II. John C. Estman of the Witherspoon Institute summarizes the situation we find ourselves in in this way:

> Our nation's elites have convinced themselves that a judicial order by a single federal court trial judge, no matter how wrong or contrary to existing precedent, is the "law of the land" and must be followed unquestioningly. . . . The ghost of the late Justice Charles Evans Hughes, who infamously said that "We are under a Constitution, but the Constitution is what the judges say it is," is undoubtedly smiling.[12]

CHRISTIANITY AND SELF-REGULATING CITIZENS

Our Founding Fathers recognized that a free society could only exist if it was made up of self-regulating citizens, and that the Christian religion was the greatest source for creating such individuals. Citizens without internal constraints on their behavior toward others require a multiplicity of laws and a police state, which was the antithesis of what they wanted to create.

GEORGE WASHINGTON

> The General hopes and trusts that every officer and man will endeavor to live and act as becomes a Christian soldier defending the dearest rights and liberties of his country.[13]

Almighty God; We make our earnest prayer that thou wilt keep the United States in thy holy protection; that thou wilt incline the hearts of the citizens to cultivate a spirit of subordination and obedience to government; and entertain a brotherly affection and love for one another and for their fellow citizens. . . . And finally that thou wilt most graciously be pleased to dispose us all to do justice, to love mercy and to demean ourselves with that charity, humility and pacific temper of mind which were the characteristics of the divine author of our blessed religion, and without a humble imitation of whose example in these things we can never hope to be a happy nation. Grant our supplication, we beseech thee, through Jesus Christ our Lord. Amen.[14]

Of all the dispositions and habits which lead to political prosperity, Religion and morality are indispensable supports. . . . Who that is a sincere friend to it, can look with indifference upon attempts to shake the foundation of the fabric? . . . And let us with caution indulge the supposition, that morality can be maintained without religion. . . . Reason and experience both forbid us to expect that National morality can prevail in exclusion of religious principle. 'Tis substantially true that virtue or morality is a necessary spring of popular government.[15]

JOHN ADAMS

We have no government armed with power capable of contenting with human passions unbridled by morality and religion. Avarice, ambition, revenge, or gallantry, would break the strongest cords of our Constitution as a whale goes through a net. Our Constitution was made only for a moral and religious people. It is wholly inadequate to the government of any other.[16]

BENJAMIN FRANKLIN

Here is my creed. I believe in one God, the Creator of the universe. That he governs it by his Providence. That he ought to be worshipped. That the most acceptable service we render to him is in doing good to his other children. That the soul of man is immortal, and will be treated with justice in another life respecting its conduct in this. These I take to be the fundamental points in all sound religion.[17]

THOMAS JEFFERSON

I, too, have made a wee-little book from the same materials, which I call the Philosophy of Jesus; it is a paradigm [a distinct set of concepts or thought patterns] of his doctrines, made by cutting the texts out of the book, and arranging them on the pages of a blank book, in a certain order of time or subject. A more beautiful or precious morsel of ethics I have never seen; it is a document in proof that *I* am a *real Christian*, that is to say, a disciple of the doctrines of Jesus, very different from the Platonists, who call *me* infidel and *themselves* Christians and preachers of the gospel, while they draw all their characteristic dogmas from what its author never said nor saw. They have compounded from the heathen mysteries a system beyond the comprehension of man.[18]

Please note that this was written prior the Restoration of the gospel—it is no wonder that he had a problem understanding the Christianity of the time.

God who gave us life gave us liberty. Can the liberties of a nation be secure when we have removed a conviction that these liberties are the gift of God? Indeed I tremble for my country when I reflect that God is just, that his justice cannot sleep forever.[19]

PATRICK HENRY

It cannot be emphasized too strongly or too often that this great nation was founded, not by religionists, but by Christians; not on religions, but on the gospel of Jesus Christ.[20]

CHAPTER SEVENTEEN

JOHN JAY, FIRST SUPREME COURT JUSTICE

> Providence has given to our people the choice of their rulers, and it is the duty as well as the privilege and interest of our Christian Nation to select and prefer Christians for their rulers.[21]

> Our laws and our institutions must necessarily be based upon and embody the teaching of the redeemer of mankind. It is impossible that they should be otherwise; and in this sense and to this extent our civilization and our institutions are emphatically Christian. . . . This is a religious people.[22]

J. CHASE

> Religion is of general and public concern, and on its support depend, in great measure, the peace and good order of government, the safety and happiness of the people. By our form of government, the Christian religion is the established religion; and all sects and denominations of Christians are placed upon the same equal footing, and are equally entitled to protection in their religious liberty.[23]

Consider also what the application of the Bill of Rights has meant to the ability of the local and state governments to control pornography. What is so wrong with each locality establishing their own standards? This was one of the purposes behind the vertical division of powers. It allows each community to set their own standards and not be dictated to by Washington, D.C. It also allows citizens to "vote with their feet" by relocating to other cities and states. The Supreme Court has removed our ability to "vote with our feet" through their activism.

You will see from the quotes below that the United States of America was founded as a Christian nation, and there is little debate about it. When the Founding Fathers talked about religion, they were referring to Christianity. What they did not want, however, was the government to favor any one Christian sect or church over the others. The necessity of the government promoting the Christian religion was considered the foundation of the government. This makes sense since you cannot have a free people who do not regulate their own behavior; those without these internal checks on their behavior need laws and police to enforce them.

THE IMPORTANCE OF CHRISTIANITY

Christianity is unique amongst the major religions of the world: let's consider Judaism, Islam, and Christianity. The first two are religions founded on "Thou Shalt Nots" (see Exodus 20:1–17), and Islam goes one step further, enforcing these "Thou Shalt Nots" vigorously through the law without any separation between religion and the government. Christianity, on the other hand, has always recognized the appropriate separation of church and state. The Savior Himself has said, "Render therefore unto Caesar the things which are Caesar's; and unto God the things that are God's" (Matthew 22:21). He also taught

> 37 *Thou shalt love the Lord* thy God with all thy heart, and with all thy soul, and with all thy mind.
> 38 This is the first and great commandment.
> 39 And the second is like unto it, *Thou shalt love thy neighbour* as thyself.
> 40 On these two commandments hang all the law [The Ten Commandments] and the prophets. (Matthew 22:37–40; emphasis added)

His religion was based upon "Thou shalt love," instead of "Thou shalt not." This makes for a large difference in the citizens of a free state. They are more concerned with doing good to others than they are about doing something bad, or even worse, about their neighbors doing something bad.

JUAN DONOSO CORTES

> [There are] only two possible forms of control: one internal and the other external; religious control and political control. They are of such a nature that when the religious barometer rises, the barometer of [external] falls and likewise, when the religious barometer

falls, the political barometer, that is political control and tyranny, rises. That is the law of humanity, a law of history. If civilized man falls into disbelief and immorality, the way is prepared for some gigantic and colossal tyrant, universal and immense.[24]

LOUIS D. BRANDEIS

The makers of our Constitution undertook to secure conditions favorable to the pursuit of happiness. They recognized the significance of man's spiritual nature, of his feelings and of his intellect. They knew that only a part of the pain, pleasure and satisfactions of life are to be found in material things. They sought to protect Americans in their beliefs, their thoughts, their emotions and their sensations. They conferred, as against the Government, the right to be let alone—the most comprehensive of rights and the right most valued by civilized men.[25]

JAMES MADISON

We have staked the whole future of American civilization, not upon the power of government, far from it. We've staked the future of all our political institutions upon our capacity . . . to sustain ourselves according to the Ten Commandments of God.[26]

JOHN ADAMS

The Christian religion is above all the Religions that ever prevailed or existed in ancient or modern times, the religion of Wisdom, Virtue, Equity, and Humanity.[27]

BENJAMIN FRANKLIN

Here is my creed: I believe in one God, the Creator of the Universe. That He governs it by His Providence. That He ought to be worshipped. That the most acceptable service we render to Him is doing good to His other children. That the soul of man is immortal, and will be treated with justice in another life, respecting its conduct in this. These I take to be the fundamental points in all sound religion. . . . As to Jesus of Nazareth, my opinion of whom you particularly desire, I think the system of morals, and his religion as he left them to us, the best the world ever saw, or is like[ly] to see.[28]

GEORGE WASHINGTON

Of all the dispositions and habits which lead to political prosperity, religion and morality are indispensable supports. In vain would that man claim the tribute of patriotism, who should labor to subvert these great pillars of human happiness, these firmest props of the duties of men and citizens. The mere politician, equally with the pious man, ought to respect and to cherish them. A volume could not trace all their connections with private and public felicity. Let it simply be asked: Where is the security for property, for reputation, for life, if the sense of religious obligation desert the oaths which are the instruments of investigation in courts of justice?[29]

While just government protects all in their religious rights, true religion affords to government its surest support.[30]

"The *Journals of the Continental Congress* clearly [declare] that the first official act of Congress upon receiving the news of the attack upon Boston by British troops was to open in prayer."[31] On September 6, 1774, Samuel Adams suggested that the first session of the first Continental Congress be opened with prayer. The motion was passed and Anglican clergy Jacob Duché was requested to come and offer the prayer. "Washington was kneeling there, and Henry, Randolph, Rutledge, Lee, and Jay, and by their side there stood, bowed in reverence, the Puritan Patriots of New England, who at that moment had reason to believe that an armed soldiery was wasting their humble households. It was believed that Boston had been bombarded and destroyed. . . . They prayed fervently 'for America, for Congress, for the Province of Massachusetts Bay, and especially for the town of Boston,' and who can realize the emotion with which they turned imploring to

Heaven for Divine Interposition—'It was enough' says Mr. Adams, 'to melt a heart of stone. I saw the tears gush into the eyes of the old, grave, pacific Quakers of Philadelphia.'"[32]

Let us now consider how people who are grounded in the Christian religion, regardless of the sect they adhere to, act, versus how people who are without religion act. I am using these two extremes to illustrate a point: without internal checks on one's own behavior, as taught by Christianity—and especially the positive, proactive elements of the first and second great commandments as taught by the Savior—the person without religion will make decisions solely based upon what is best for them in the moment, and with little or no thought for the well-being, feelings, or rights of others.

Let's continue to use my extreme example knowing that those without religion will not act this way all the time, as much as those professing Christ act accordingly all the time. We are looking for the natural tendencies of these individuals, and how we would expect them to act most of the time. A member of Congress would either be out for her own grandizement, power, and financial gain, or she would be there to serve her fellow citizens by respecting their rights. A police officer would either be puffed up with the power he exercises over others, or he would recognize that he is a servant and employee of the people and would treat them accordingly. A district attorney would either be out to make a name for herself to promote her political aspirations without respect for the rights of the accused, or she would be out to serve justice. The judge would either be prideful due to his power and out to make the law into what he thinks it should be, or he would respect the democratic process that created the law and would interpret it accordingly. I am oversimplifying here, but I think you can see my point. There must be internal constraints on those in political positions, or situational ethics will take over and the natural man will be exhibited at the expense of other citizens.

I include, in part, the speech, "What Made America Great," delivered to the House of Representative in 2001:

The key phrase we now use, which first appeared in the judicial vocabulary in the United States in 1947, is the separation of church and state. . . .

The logic behind this phrase is that religion is a private matter that should neither guide nor even be allowed to possibly influence public education, the formation of minds, government legislation, the formation of laws, and judicial rulings on what is legal and just, the maintenance of justice. These are seen as distinctly secular arenas. Religion as a living force must be kept out of any public process that is in any way supported by any level of local, State or federal funds. . . .

A few historic and generic references to God are still allowed. Our coins still say "in God we trust," a statement put there by the United States Congress to remind Americans of the true source of their security.

Our Supreme Court and the Houses of Congress still invoke the name of God. Presidents are still inaugurated with their hand on the Bible when taking the oath of office. . . .

But each of these traditions is already under attack, and in America today to teach that the great laws and principles of the Judeo-Christian heritage and the morality of the Bible were the unique bases of our national government and offer the guiding norm for our Nation is now an illegal act.

In our day, this American concept of freedom is now defined as the freedom to say anything, show anything, believe or promote anything, and act in any way, with no submission to regard or even respect toward any concept of a guiding prescriptive truth or morality.

There is only one kind of freedom of speech the first amendment no longer protects in this new era; that is prayer. . . .

Academic freedom has become the freedom of student or teacher to hold or express views against any national organization or patriotic, moral or religious principle without fear of arbitrary interference, except if the student is deemed bigoted, homophobic, chauvinistic, anti-feministic, imperialistic, police-raid patriotic, religious, politically conservative or otherwise politically incorrect. Then he must be shamed.

The only sacred virtue that is still taught in our secular universities, one that must be protected, is absolute tolerance towards all views and lifestyles as equally valid, valuable and honorable, except any faith-based moral view that challenges that assumption. Then absolute intolerance toward that person is a virtue. . . .

Bartlett continues,

To allow the Christian faith to shape the public arena is now condemned as unconstitutional. . . . Since then, our children are taught . . . that the Founding Fathers were primarily atheists or deists. . . .

Actually, 52 of the 55 signers of the Declaration of Independence were orthodox, deeply-committed Christians. The other three all believed in the Bible as divine truth, the God of scripture, and his personal intervention. . . .

Now to the man that historical revisionists most often claim was a deist. . . . Was Benjamin Franklin a deist?

This is what [Benjamin Franklin] said: *"In the days of our contest with Great Britain when we were sensible of danger, we had daily prayer in this room for divine protection. Our prayers, sir, were heard, and they were graciously answered. . . . To that kind providence we owe this happy opportunity to establish our Nation. And have we now forgotten that powerful friend? Do we imagine that we no longer need his assistance? . . . I therefore beg leave to move that henceforth prayers imploring the assistance of heaven and its blessings on our deliberations be held in this assembly every morning before we proceed to any business."*

The following year, in a letter to the French Minister of State, Franklin, speaking of our Nation, said, *"Whoever shall introduce into public office the principles of Christianity will change the face of the world." . . .*

Bartlett, speaking of the Constitution's vitality, continues:

At the time of our Nation's bicentennial in 1976, political science professors at the University of Houston began to ask some key questions: *Why is it that the American Constitution has been able to stand the test of time? . . .* They spent 10 years cataloging 15,000 documents of the Founding Fathers. . . .

34 percent of all of the quotes and the writings of the Founding Fathers were direct word-for-word quotes from the Bible. Further, another 60 percent of their quotes were quoting men who were quoting the Bible, so that an incredible 94 percent of all of the quotes in these 15,000 documents were direct quotes from or references to the Bible.

So how did they produce a document that has withstood the test of an evolving government and growing Nation for 225 years? The answer: these men were steeped in the word of God. . . .

These leaders knew their Bible, and they absolutely trusted its wisdom. *So the first great lie in America today is that our Founding Fathers were not Christians seeking to establish a Christian Nation. They most decidedly were.*

The second lie emerges from the first. It is that the Founding Fathers established a wall of separation between religion, especially Christianity and government, to ensure that these two would not mix. . . . Here is the truth: . . . [the intent of the Founding Fathers] *was to establish a distinctly Christian Nation, but one where no one Christian denomination ruled over the other denominations, as had been the case in so much of Europe. They wanted to honor the fact that under God, all men are created equal in value and rights. . . .*

Regardless of how we feel about it today, the historical fact is that there was no separation of church and state, other than a lack of government funding of one denomination for 160 years of American history. They were one and the same. The first amendment did not separate religion from government; it simply ensured that no one denomination was favored over all others, as in England.

And he continues:

In *March 27, 1854, Senate Committee on the Judiciary chair*, Senator Badger, issued its final report. Let me quote from this resolution: . . .

"In this age there can be no substitute for Christianity. By its general principles, the Christian faith is the great conserving element on which we must rely for the purity and permanence of our free institutions." . . .

How do we get from where we were for two centuries to where we are in 2001?

First . . . in 1947, the Supreme Court in Everson vs. Board of Education deviated from every precedent for the first time and in a limited way affirmed a wall of separation between church and State in the public classroom. . . .

Then in 1962 . . . in Engle vs. Vitale, the Supreme Court removed prayer from public schools. . . .

Then things happened fast. On June 17, 1963, the Supreme Court ruled in Abington vs. Schemp that Bible reading was outlawed as unconstitutional in the public school system. . . .

In 1965, the Courts denied as unconstitutional the right of a student in the public school cafeteria to bow his head and pray audibly for his food. . . . In 1980, Stone vs. Graham outlawed the Ten Commandments in our public school system. . . .

Now we have an entire population that has no clue of its true American heritage. They have not forgotten; they have never known or heard the truth of our founding as a Christian Nation.[33]

NOTES

1. James Madison, Bill of Rights, proposed provision, http://law2.umkc.edu /faculty/projects/ftrials/conlaw/billofrightsintro.html.
2. W. Cleon Skousen, *The Making of America: The Substance and Meaning of the Constitution* (Washington, D.C.: National Center for Constitutional Studies, 1985).

3. Andrew Jackson, "Message from the President of the United States, Returning the Bank Bill to the Senate with His Objections, July 10, 1832," in *Annual Messages, Veto Messages Protest, etc. of Andrew Jackson, President of the United States* (Baltimore: Edward J. Coale and Co., 1835), 236.

4. James H. Fowler and Sangick Jeon, "The Authority of Supreme Court Precedent," *Social Networks* 30 (2008): 16; http://fowler.ucsd.edu /authority_of_supreme_court_precedent.pdf.

5. Ibid.; 16–17.

6. Ibid.

7. Robert H. Bork, *Coercing Virtue: The Worldwide Rule of Judges* (Washington, D.C.: AEI Press, 2003), 70–71.

8. Archibald Cox, *The Role of the Supreme Court in American Government* (New York: Oxford, 1976), 54, 113–14.

9. Alexander M. Bickel, *The Morality of Consent* (New Haven: Yale, 1975), 27–29.

10. Andrew Jackson, "Message from the President of the United States, Returning the Bank Bill to the Senate with His Objections, July 10, 1832," in *Annual Messages, Veto Messages Protest, etc. of Andrew Jackson, President of the United States* (Baltimore: Edward J. Coale and Co., 1835), 236.

11. Letter from Thomas Jefferson to Edward Livingston, March 1825.

12. John C. Eastman, "Federal Court Precedent: A Defense of Judge Roy Moore and the Alabama Supreme Court," *The Witherspoon Institute*, March 16, 2015, http://www.thepublicdiscourse.com/2015/03/14627/. See also The Heritage Foundation at www.heritage.org for more information regarding judicial activism.

13. George Washington, "General Orders, Head Quarters, New York, July 9, 1776," in Michael A. Shea, *In God We Trust: George Washington and the Spiritual Destiny of the United States of America* (Derry, News Hampshire, Liberty Quest, 2012).

14. George Washington, "Washington's Prayer," in *A Prayer Book for the Public and Private Use of Our Soldiers and Sailors* (Philadelphia: Bishop White Prayer Book Society, 1917), 104.

15. George Washington, Farewell Address, September 19, 1796.

16. Letter from John Adams to Massachusetts Militia, October 1798.

17. Benjamin Franklin, quoted in Benjamin F. Morris, *The Christian Life and Character of the Civil Institutions of the United States* (Powder Springs, Georgia: American Vision, 2007), 157–58.

18. Letter from Thomas Jefferson to Charles Thomson, 1816.

19. Jefferson Memorial, Panel 3, Washington, D.C.

20. Patrick Henry, quoted in Hanna Rosin, *God's Harvard: A Christian College on a Mission to Save America* (New York: Harcourt, 2007), 116.

21. United States of America Congressional Record: Proceedings and Debates of the 108th Congress First Session, vol. 149, part 15 (Washington, D.C.: United States Government Printing Office, 2003), 21335.

22. Ibid.; 21336.

23. J. Chase, Runkel vs. Winemiller, October 1799, in Thomas Harris and John McHenry, *Maryland Reports, Being a Series of the Most Important Law Cases Argued and Determined in the General Court and Court of Appeals of the State of Maryland*, vol. 4 (Annapolis: Jonas Green, 1818), 450.

24. Juan Donoso Cortes, quoted in Michael Freeden, Lyman Tower Sargent, and Marc Stears, eds., *The Oxford Handbook of Political Ideologies* (Oxford: Oxford University Press, 2013), 294.

25. Olmstead vs. United States, 277 US 438, 1928.

26. James Madison, to the General Assembly of the State of Virginia, 1778.

27. John Adams, personal diary, July 26, 1796.

28. Letter from Benjamin Franklin to Ezra Stiles, March 1790.

29. George Washington, Farewell Address, September 19, 1796.

30. Letter from George Washington to The Synod of the Dutch Reformed Church in North America, 1789.

31. Kelly Gneiting, "The First Prayer in the Continental Congress, Have We Such Men of Faith Today?," *Independent American Party*, August 26, 2015.

32. Placard Summarizing the Founders' Reports Concerning the Impact of That First Prayer, on Kelly Gneiting, "The First Prayer in the Continental Congress, Have We Such Men of Faith Today?," *Independent American Party*, August 26, 2015.

33. Representative Roscoe Bartlett of Maryland to the House of Representatives, October 17, 2001, "What Made America Great," www.congress.gov; emphasis added.

EIGHTEEN

Conclusion

SAMUEL ADAMS

> If ye love wealth better than liberty, the tranquility of servitude better than the animating contest of freedom—go from us in peace. We ask not your counsel nor your arms. Crouch down and lick the hand that feeds you. May your chains sit lightly upon you, and may posterity forget that ye were our countrymen![1]

Without the Savior's religion being accepted by our national government, we have the problems mentioned by Representative Boscoe Bartlett above, just as we were warned by the Savior through Moroni:

> 7 And the Lord would not suffer that they should stop beyond the sea in the wilderness, but he would that they should come forth even unto the land of promise, which was choice above all other lands, which the Lord God had preserved for a righteous people.
> 8 And he had sworn in his wrath unto the brother of Jared, that whoso should possess this land of promise, from that time henceforth and forever, should serve him, the true and only God, or they should be swept off when the fulness of his wrath should come upon them.

9 And now, we can behold the decrees of God concerning this land, that it is a land of promise; and whatsoever nation shall possess it shall serve God, or they shall be swept off when the fulness of his wrath shall come upon them. And the fulness of his wrath cometh upon them when they are ripened in iniquity.

10 For behold, this is a land which is choice above all other lands; wherefore he that doth possess it shall serve God or shall be swept off; for it is the everlasting decree of God. And it is not until the fulness of iniquity among the children of the land, that they are swept off.

11 And this cometh unto you, O ye Gentiles, that ye may know the decrees of God—that ye may repent, and not continue in your iniquities until the fulness come, that ye may not bring down the fulness of the wrath of God upon you as the inhabitants of the land have hitherto done.

12 Behold, this is a choice land, and whatsoever nation shall possess it shall be free from bondage, and from captivity, and from all other nations under heaven, if they will but serve the God of the land, who is Jesus Christ, who hath been manifested by the things which we have written. (Ether 2:7–12)

The philosophy of the Founding Fathers can be summarized using the words of Henry David "There will never be a really free and enlightened State until the State comes to recognize the individual as a higher and independent power, from which all its own power and authority are derived, and treats him accordingly."[2]

JOSIAH QUINCY JR.

Blandishments will not fascinate us, nor will threats of a "halter" intimidate. For under God, we are determined that wheresoever, whensoever, or howsoever, we shall be called to make our exit, we will die freemen.[3]

WILLIAM PITT

Necessity is the argument of tyrants; it is the creed of slaves.[4]

Our Founding Fathers' love for liberty, and the responsibility that they felt toward passing it on to their posterity, is clearly indicated in the following quotations:

SAMUEL ADAMS

The liberties of our Country, the freedom of our civil constitution are worth defending at all hazards: And it is our duty to defend them against all attacks. We have receiv'd [sic] them as a fair Inheritance from our worthy Ancestors: They have purchas'd [sic] them for us with toil and danger and expence [sic] of treasure and blood; and transmitted them to us with care and diligence. It will bring an everlasting mark of infamy on the present generation, enlightened as it is, if we should suffer them to be wrested from us by violence without a struggle; or be cheated out of them by the artifices of false and designing men. Of the latter we are in most danger at present: Let us therefore be aware of it. Let us contemplate our forefathers and posterity; and resolve to maintain the rights bequeath'd [sic] to us from the former, for the sake of the latter. . . . Let us remember, that "if we suffer tamely a lawless attack upon our liberty, we encourage it, and involve others in our doom." It is a very serious consideration, which should deeply impress our minds, that *millions yet unborn may be the miserable sharers of the event.*[5]

DANIEL WEBSTER

God grants liberty only to those who love it, and are always ready to guard and defend it.[6]

WINSTON CHURCHILL

If you will not fight for right when you can easily win without bloodshed; if you will not fight when your victory will be sure and not too costly; you may come to the moment when you will have to fight with all odds against you and only a precarious chance of survival. There may be even a worse fate. You may have to fight when there is no hope of victory, because it is better to perish than to live as slaves.[7]

Having been given this tremendous blessing of liberty, this should be our motto: "To be born a free man is a blessing; To live as a free man is a responsibility; To die as a free man is an obligation" (anonymous). What are you doing to help America return to its founding principles?

ELMER DAVIS

This will remain the land of the free only so long as it is the home of the brave.[8]

THOMAS JEFFERSON

A bill of rights is what the people are entitled to against every government on earth, general or particular; and what no just government should refuse, or rest on inference.[9]

SAMUEL ADAMS

Among the natural rights of the colonists are these: First, a right to life; Secondly, to liberty; Thirdly, to property; together with the right to support and defend them in the best manner they can.[10]

LOUIS D. BRANDEIS

They [the makers of the Constitution] conferred, as against the Government, the right to be let alone—the most comprehensive of rights and the right most valued by civilized men.[11]

GROVER CLEVELAND

There is no calamity which a great nation can invite which equals that which follows from a supine submission to wrong and injustice, and the consequent loss of national self-respect and honor, beneath which are shielded and defended a people's safety and greatness.[12]

ALEXANDER HAMILTON

Every man is bound to answer these questions to himself, according to the best of his conscience and understanding, and to act agreeably to the genuine and sober dictates of his judgment. This is a duty from which nothing can give him a dispensation. 'T is one that he is called upon, nay, constrained by all the obligations that form the bands of society, to discharge sincerely and honestly. No partial motive, no particular interest, no pride of opinion, no temporary passion or prejudice, will justify to himself, to his country, or to his posterity, an improper election of the part he is to act. Let him beware of an obstinate adherence to party; let him reflect that the object upon which he is to decide is not a particular interest of the community, but the very existence of the nation.[13]

THOMAS PAINE

Moderation in temper is always a virtue; but moderation in principle is always a vice.[14]

It may be of value to reread Patrick Henry's famous speech in the House of Burgesses, Virginia, 1775:

It is natural to man to indulge in the illusions of hope. We are apt to shut our eyes against a painful truth. . . . Is this the part of wise men, engaged in a great and arduous struggle for liberty? Are we disposed to be of the number of those who, having eyes, see not, and having ears, hear not, the things which so nearly concern their temporal salvation? For my part, whatever anguish of spirit it may cost, I am willing to know the whole truth; to know the worst and to provide for it. I have but one lamp by which my feet are guided; and that is the lamp of experience. I know of no way of judging of the future but by the past . . . we shall not fight our battles alone. There is a just God who presides over the destinies of nations; and who will raise up friends to fight our battles for us. . . . There is no retreat, but in submission and slavery! Our chains are forged! Their clanking may be heard on the plains of Boston! The war is inevitable—and let it come! I repeat it, sir, let it come! . . . Gentlemen may cry peace, peace—but there is no peace. The war is actually begun! . . . Is life so dear, or peace so sweet, as to be purchased at the price of chains and slavery? Forbid it, Almighty God! I know not what course others may take; but as for me, give me liberty or give me death![15]

BRIGHAM YOUNG

Protect and sustain civil and religious liberty and *every constitutional right*.[16]

How long will it be before the words of the prophet Joseph will be fulfilled? He said *if the Constitution of the United States were saved at all* it must be done by this people.[17]

When the *Constitution . . . hangs*, as it were, upon a single *thread*, they will have to call for the "Mormon" Elders to save it from utter destruction; and they will step forth and do it.[18]

Will the *Constitution* be destroyed? No: it will be held inviolate by this people; and, as Joseph Smith said, "The time will come when the destiny of the nation will hang upon a single *thread* [the original quotation of Joseph Smith does not mention the *Constitution*]. At that critical juncture, this people will step forth and save it from the threatened destruction." It will be so.[19]

J. REUBEN CLARK, JR.

You and I have heard all our lives that the time may come when the *Constitution* may hang by a *thread*. I do not know whether it is a *thread*, or a small rope by which it *now hangs*, but I do know that whether it shall live or die is now in the balance.[20]

Elder Orson Hyde recalled a slightly different wording of Joseph Smith's alleged statement regarding the Constitution than did some of Hyde's contemporaries:

It is said that brother Joseph in his lifetime declared that the Elders of this Church should step forth at a particular time when the Constitution should be in danger, and rescue it, and save it. This may be so; but I do not recollect that he said exactly so. I believe he said something like this—that *the time would come when the Constitution and the country would be in danger of an overthrow*; and said he, *If the Constitution be saved at all, it will be by the Elders of this Church*. I believe this is about the language, as nearly as I can recollect it.[21]

In conclusion, I strongly recommend you read the Declaration of Independence, the Constitution, and "The Proper Role of Government," by Ezra Taft Benson. President Benson was not only the President of the Church, but he was also quite familiar with the government, and served a cabinet-level position in the Eisenhower administration. He was uniquely qualified to speak on the proper role of government, both from a spiritual standpoint and a secular one; he had direct, internal experience with the way government functions.

May we be willing to reconsider our political ideals—the philosophies of men—in relation to their use of force on our fellow citizens, and see the importance of liberty in all its splendor for the education of our eternal souls, including the pain we experience from our bad decisions. Any governmental action which tries to shield us from experiencing the pain of our decisions is contrary to His eternal purposes, and are "more of less than this" and "cometh of evil."

NOTES

1. Steve Coffman, ed., *Words of the Founding Fathers: Selected Quotations from Franklin, Washington, Adams, Jefferson, Madison, and Hamilton* (Jefferson, North Carolina: McFarland & Company, 2012), 156.
2. Henry David Thoreau, *Civil Disobedience* (1849).
3. M. Laird Simons, ed., *Cyclopaedia of American Literature* (Philadelphia: Baxter Publishing, 1881), 1:262.

4. Carroll D. Wright, ed., *The New Century Book of Facts: A Handbook of Ready Reference* (Springfield, Massachusetts: The King-Richardson Company, 1909), 960.

5. Harry Alonzo Cushing ed., *The Writings of Samuel Adams* (New York: G. P. Putnam's Sons, 1906), 2:255–56; emphasis in original.

6. Daniel Webster, speech, June 3, 1834, in William J. Federer, *America's God and Country: Encyclopedia of Quotations* (St. Louis: Amerisearch, 2000), 670.

7. Winston Churchill, quoted in Thomas Lake, *Romans 13 In a Constitutional Republic* (2011), 46.

8. Elmer Davis, *But We Were Born Free* (Bobbs-Merrill, 1954), 115.

9. Letter from Thomas Jefferson to James Madison, December 1787.

10. "The Rights of the Colonists," *Constitution Society*, 1772, last updated February 6, 2017, www.constitution.org/bcp/right_col.htm.

11. Olmstead vs. United States, 277 U.S. 438, 1928.

12. Message to Congress, December 17, 1895, quoted in Robert Kagan, *Dangerous Nation* (New York: Vintage Books, 2007), 372.

13. Federalist Papers, no. 85.

14. John P. Kaminski ed., *Citizen Paine: Thomas Paine's Thoughts on Man, Government, Society, and Religion* (New York: Rowman & Littlefield Publishers, 2002), 154.

15. Lewis Copeland, Lawrence W. Lamm, and Stephen J. McKenna eds., *The World's Great Speeches*, 4th ed. (New York: Dover Publications, 1997), 232–34.

16. Brigham Young, in *Journal of Discourses*, 2:263; emphasis added.

17. Brigham Young, in *Journal of Discourses*, 12:204; emphasis added.

18. Brigham Young, in *Journal of Discourses*, 2:182; emphasis added.

19. Brigham Young, in *Journal of Discourses*, 2:15; emphasis added.

20. J. Reuben Clark, in Conference Report, October 1942, 58; emphasis added.

21. Orson Hyde, in *Journal of Discourses*, 6:152; emphasis added.

About the Author

Morris Harmor was born and raised in Pittsford, New York. He was baptized with his family in the Cumorah Mission of The Church of Jesus Christ of Latter-day Saints when he was twelve years old. After graduating from the State University of New York at Geneseo, he taught as a science teacher and ultimately found his way into selling computer-aided design, manufacturing, and engineering software.

While growing up, he learned about his father's concerns regarding the US Constitution. Since that time, he has read numerous biographies on the Founding Fathers and several books about American history and the Constitution in an effort to understand the original intent of the Founding Fathers. He has also studied the scriptures in an effort to determine correct political positions that would be in harmony with the Lord's will.

Photo Courtesy of Teagan Condie.